SHELL GUIDES

edited by JOHN BETJEMAN AND JOHN PIPER

CORNWALL
John Betjeman

DORSET
Michael Pitt-Rivers

THE ISLE OF WIGHT
C. J. Pennethorne-Hughes

LINCOLNSHIRE
Henry Thorold and Jack Yates

NORFOLK
Wilhelmine Harrod and C. L. S. Linnell

RUTLAND
W. G. Hoskins

SOUTH-WEST WALES
PEMBROKESHIRE AND CARMARTHENSHIRE
Vyvyan Rees

SUFFOLK
Norman Scarfe

WORCESTERSHIRE
James Lees-Milne

---

edited by JOHN PIPER

ESSEX
Norman Scarfe

GLOUCESTERSHIRE
David Verey

KENT
C. J. Pennethorne-Hughes

LEICESTERSHIRE
W. G. Hoskins

MID-WESTERN WALES
CARDIGANSHIRE AND MERIONETH
Vyvyan Rees

NORTHUMBERLAND
Thomas Sharp

NORTH WALES
Elisabeth Beazley and Lionel Brett

WILTSHIRE
J. H. Cheetham and John Piper

NORTHAMPTONSHIRE
Juliet Smith

THE SHELL PILOT TO THE SOUTH COAST HARBOURS
K. Adlard Coles

A Shell Guide

Mid Western Wales
Cardiganshire and Merioneth

The shimmer and sparkle of white walls through leaves, and among vivid
green fields, give constant pleasure to the traveller in Wales. Doors and
window-frames of the white farms and barns are often black, and another old
favourite is the colour that paint manufacturers used to call
'mid-purple-brown'; but these often give place now to gay and jaunty
colours, according to local fancy. And long may gaiety reign here over
'propriety' and so-called 'good taste'.

A Shell Guide

Mid Western Wales
Cardiganshire and Merioneth

by Vyvyan Rees

Faber & Faber 3 Queen Square London

First published in 1971
by Faber and Faber Limited
3 Queen Square London WC1
Printed in Great Britain by
Shenval Press, London and Harlow
All rights reserved

ISBN 0 571 09642 5

Contents

List of illustrations   6

Cardiganshire: Introduction   9

Cardiganshire: Gazetteer   29

Merioneth: Introduction   77

Merioneth: Gazetteer   93

Index   141

Acknowledgements

There is hardly a parish in these counties without someone to whom my thanks are due, whether he or she be the owner of a house visited, the parson or minister, the local roadman, policeman, publican or postman. Their contributions to the information collected for this volume are too numerous to mention. So too is the help of local councils and other bodies at all levels. I hope it is not invidious to mention specially the National Library of Wales and the officials of the Merioneth Historical and Record Society and the County Archivist, Mr Lloyd Hughes.

I also have a special debt to the editor of this series, Mr John Piper. His kindness, sympathy and patience have been of more help to me than I can say.

If I am allowed a dedication it is to my fellow countrymen of the uplands of Wales, who in a phrase which lingers in my memory and I cannot locate "live under the hem of God's skirt".

Vyvyan Rees
Dinas, Pembrokeshire.
Cheltenham, Glos.

Illustrations

Front endpaper
Artists' Valley
John Piper
Devil's Bridge
Peter Burton

Frontispiece
Farm near Tregroes
John Piper

Title page
Talyllyn railway locomotive
E. Emrys Jones

CARDIGANSHIRE INTRODUCTION

Page
 8 Plinlimon
John Piper

10/11 Between Tregaron Bog
and the Great Desert
John Piper

12 Between Tregaron and
Abergwesin
John Piper

14 Near New Quay
Peter Burton

15 Near Llangranog
Roger Mayne
Cwmtudu
Peter Burton

16 Llansaintffraid
John Piper

17 Aberystwyth
John Piper

18 Between Tregaron and
Llanddewi Brefi
John Piper

19 Llangeitho
John Piper

20 Near Ponterwyd
Above Bont-rhyd-y-beddau
Above Talybont
John Piper

21 Abergwesin Pass
John Piper
Below Nant y Moch
John Piper

22 Ystwyth Valley, Manor House,
Abermad
John Piper

23 Hafod
Edwin Smith
Bronwydd
John Piper

Page
24 Cross Inn, Ffair-rhos,
Pontrhydfendigaid
Llanddewi Brefi
John Piper

25 Near Blaenpennal
Llansaintffraid, Cross Inn
John Piper

26 Llansaintffraid,
Llanon Methodist Chapel
John Piper

27 Bethesda, Llanddewi Brefi
John Piper

CARDIGANSHIRE GAZETTEER

Page
30 Aberaeron
G. Douglas Bolton

31 Aberystwyth, war memorial
John Piper

32 Aberystwyth
Peter Burton

33 Aberystwyth,
University College
John Piper

33 Aberystwyth
Peter Burton

34/35 Llyn Fanod, Blaenpennal
John Piper

36 Cardigan bridge
Peter Burton

37 Cardigan market hall
John Piper

39 Lampeter
John Piper

41 Lampeter
John Piper

42 Lampeter
John Piper

43 Llanafan, Trawscoed garden
John Piper

45 Llanbadarn y Creuddyn Lower,
stables at Nanteos
John Piper

46 Llanddewi Brefi
John Piper

49 Llanfihangel y Creuddyn Lower
John Piper

50 Llanfihangel y Creuddyn Upper,
Devil's Bridge Valley
John Piper

Page
51 Devil's Bridge,
Falls of the Mynach
John Piper & Roger Mayne

53 Llangeitho
John Piper

56 Llangybi, Derry Ormond Tower
John Piper

58 Llantyssiliogogo, Cwmtudu
Peter Burton

59 Coybal Bay near New Quay
Peter Burton

60 Llanwenog
John Piper

61 Melindwr, Goginan
John Piper

62 Orllwyn, Penrhiwllan
John Piper

63 Fainc Ddu, Plinlimon
John Piper

64 Pontrhydfendigaid
John Piper

65 Pontrhydfendigaid, tombstone
at Strata Florida
John Piper

66 Strata Florida abbey
John Piper

67 Strata Florida
John Piper

69 Pontrhydfendigaid, Llyn Teifi
John Piper

70 Troedyraur lychgate
John Piper

71 Ysgubor y Coed, Eglwysfach
Peter Burton

72 Yspytty Ystwyth, Pontrhydygroes
John Piper

73 "Salem", a painting by S. C.
Vosper. Reproduced by
courtesy of the Lady Lever Art
Gallery, Port Sunlight

74 Village memorials
John Piper

75 War memorials
John Piper

MERIONETH INTRODUCTION

Page

76 Craig yr Aderyn
John Piper

77 Tomen y mur, near Trawsfynydd
John Piper

78 Blaenau Ffestiniog
John Piper

79 Corris
John Piper

80 Llanfachreth
John Piper

81 Bala Lake
John Piper

83 Cader Idris
John Piper
Llyn Du
John Piper

84 Craig y Pant, Bwlch y Groes
John Piper

86 Dolgellau
Corris
John Piper

87 Blaenau Ffestiniog
Edwin Smith

89 Harlech Castle
Edwin Smith

90 The Mawddach Estuary
Roger Mayne

91 The Glaslyn Estuary
Peter Burton

92 The Manod, near Ffestiniog
Edwin Smith

MERIONETH GAZETTEER

Page

93 Aberdovey
Merioneth Historical Society

94 Aran Mawddwy
John Piper

95 Aran Benllyn
John Piper

96 Arenigs
John Piper
Llyn Arenig Fawr
John Piper

98 Barmouth
Peter Burton

99 Barmouth
G. Douglas Bolton

100 Brithdir, altar, detail
John Piper

101 Brithdir altar
John Piper

102 Brithdir church
John Piper

103 Llanfachreth
John Piper

105 Cader Idris, Llyn Cau
John Piper

107 Corwen
E. Emrys Jones

108/109 Dolgellau
John Piper

110 Llyn Stwlan, reservoir
John Piper

111 Ffestiniog
Blaenau Ffestiniog
John Piper

Page

112/113 Blaenau Ffestiniog
John Piper & Roger Mayne

114 Harlech
Edwin Smith

117 Dovecote at Tyfos, Llandderfel
John Piper

119 Llanegryn
John Piper

121 Llanelltud, Cymmer Abbey
Peter Burton

122 Llanfachreth
John Piper

127 Llanymawddwy
John Piper

129 Portmeirion
Edwin Smith

130 Rhinog: the Roman Steps
John Piper

132 Rhinog Fach: Llyn y bo and
the Rhobells
John Piper

133 Rhinog Fawr
Llyn Hywel
John Piper

135 Corris
John Piper

136 Corris
John Piper

138 Towyn
Merioneth Historical Society

Back endpaper
Blaenau Ffestiniog
Roger Mayne

Cardiganshire: **Introduction**

The sense of remoteness is stronger in Cardiganshire than in any other seaward county of Wales. Here is a landscape of constantly changing shape and colour. There is an unawareness of urgency: this is a pastoral "undeveloped" land.

The county is shaped like a crescent moon whose upper tip is at Aberystwyth and its lower at Cardigan, with Cardigan Bay and the Cambrian Mountains bounding its flanks. Sheltered thus from the east and north and open to the mild seaborne air, the gently undulating countryside of the central ridges and plateaus has a rich green look except where it is devoid of natural drainage and there are sour tracts of swamp and moorland, marginal land,

> "where flesh meets spirit
> only on Sundays, and the days between
> are mortgaged to the grasping soil."

The only industry is agriculture; there are no aerodromes, no factory chimneys, no Defence Establishments except at Aberporth. The hydro-electric complex fed from the Nant y Moch reservoir enhances the landscape. The coastline is dotted with small ports once busy with ship-building and coastwise traffic, and now regaining a measure of prosperity from tourist trade.

Four rivers cross the county from the Plinlimon range to Cardigan Bay. The richest and most varied is the Teifi. It rises in one of a cluster of lakes in rock-strewn moorland north of Tregaron, and flows south in the lee of the Cambrian Mountains to Llandyssul where it turns west and forms the county southern boundary to the sea. At convenient places a series of small market towns, Newcastle Emlyn (actually in Carmarthenshire), Llandyssul, Lampeter and Tregaron have their roots deep in the past below their 19th-century crust. There are places of great natural beauty, contained in a

close setting, between Llandyssul and Cardigan among the river's deep pools and fast shallows, notably the gorge at Henllan, the falls at Cenarth and in the wooded ravine below Cilgerran Castle. Teifi salmon and sewin (a species of sea trout) are famous, and coracle fishermen can be seen at Cenarth. The river is reputedly the last haunt of the beaver in Britain. With its tributaries, it supplied power for a once thriving woollen industry of which the only surviving mills are at Llandyssul, Capel Dewi and Maesllyn.

Northward and through the heart of the county, the Aeron valley is tenderly beautiful, wooded and pastured like a great park between the gently receding hills. Beyond Llangeitho it flows from its source in the swamps around Llyn Fanod through desolate, marginal land. The Ystwyth river drains into the sea at Aberystwyth, meandering past deserted mine workings, rich native woodland, and forest plantations. Roughly parallel to it, the Rheidol, eager to outstrip the others in its race to the sea, is the most picturesque; it has inspired painters and poets, and sightseers flock to it. Here John Nash, little more than a master builder down on his luck in Carmarthen, absorbed, under the patronage of the Johnes family of Hafod and their friend Uvedale Price, the latter's theory of the Picturesque, which was later to find expression in Nash's romantically sited buildings.

The middle reaches of the Rheidol presage the changing character of the landscape northwards to the Dovey estuary, which forms the county's northern boundary. The hills encroach more steeply on flat marshy land at sea level; the woodlands on their western protected flanks are denser and more luxuriant. Minor valleys of great beauty, Leri, Ceulan, Clettwr, Einion and Llyfnant are little more than ravines through dense woodland, and where there is traffic access through them to their moorland heads, it is by narrow lanes, high along their flanks. Thus at the county's northern boundary, the gradation is

From the summit of
PLINLIMON, looking north

Between Tregaron Bog and the Great Desert

completed from the pasture land of Carmarthenshire to the rugged crags and peaks of north Wales.

From the ribbed land in the centre, beyond the upper reaches of the Teifi and east and north of Strata Florida and Tregaron, lies the Great Desert of Wales, vast, barely inhabited moorland broken by ravines and outcrops of rocks with dark, peaty lakes. On a still winter's day the silence is absolute; in the spring and early summer it is sweetly broken by the cries of lapwings and curlews, in whom the Welsh legends say that the spirits of witches have lodged. The Desert stretches eastwards towards Rhayadr, much of it opened since the last war. Miles of roads have been constructed which mostly follow the old drovers' cattle trails to the markets and fatter pastures of England. The Forestry Commission needs these roads for the planting, tending and harvesting of millions of trees, and the water authorities need them for the building and servicing of the reservoirs. They are making many of their own roads and the most spectacular and useful to the public are those across the Desert into Montgomeryshire. The Abergwesin Mountain Road to Tregaron has been in use for some time, and there is now another route from Llanddewi Brefi to Rhayadr, and an even newer one from Nant y Moch lake near Plinlimon westward to Talybont, near the sea. This traverses the fairly tame uplands, planted by the Forestry Commission with young

trees, for some miles, and then begins the grand long valley-side descent from the open moorland passing the modest, near-mountain hafod, or summer, farms and then reaching, as it descends, the gradually more prosperous, tree-planted lands, further and further down the Ceulan valley. A road with very similar features, but un-metalled, has been laid by the Forestry Commission through the Glasffrwd valley over the Desert to join the Tregaron Mountain Road.

There are other new tracks now passable for cars, though care is needed, sometimes skill, and sometimes even temerity (along which wayfaring men, though fools, should not err) such as the track towards Plinlimon from Ponterwyd, near the Dyffryn Castle Hotel, that ends near Nant y Moch lake or the track south of the Leri ravine in Tirymynach parish.

There are other, smaller deserts, shores of the Dead Sea in miniature where the earth, drained of her wealth in lead and silver, has been left grey with slag heaps, on which nothing grows and the crumbling masonry of abandoned buildings casts its shadows.

The Forestry Commission, besides opening up the mountain deserts, will inevitably alter their character, the appeal of their wide horizons and the play of sunlight and shadow on the bare slopes. The lapwings and curlews will find new haunts. The plantations, in the upper reaches of the Towy, east of Tregaron, will become one of the largest forests of Wales, employing a much

larger labour force than the few farmsteads and sheep holdings. The great Ystwyth Forest covers over five hundred acres around Pontrhydygroes along the deep ravines and is bordered by native trees, cherry, oak and beech. Plantations on their uncultivated higher slopes, as at Nantyrarian in the Rheidol valley, do not diminish the beauty of the wider valleys.

In the uplands there is little evidence of community life; villages are hardly more than hamlets or church and chapel groups on the through, roller coaster roads. The mountains lack the grandeur of those to the north. Plinlimon, nondescript in outline, rises to about 2,400 feet and, of the others, Tregaron alone (1,778 feet) exceeds 1,500 feet. As to the two great bogs, Cors Tregaron is scheduled as a Nature Reserve and Borth is now partly under cultivation. The A and B class roads are good and fast, the B class particularly so and traffic-free even at the height of summer.

Megaliths and dolmens are a feature of the promontories below and above Cardigan Bay, but not in it. The earliest traces in stone of prehistory are the few cairns which dot the uplands, and are generally associated with the Bronze Age. The ridge between the Cellan and Twrch valleys above Llanfair Clydogau is a good place to look for them. There are few Iron Age hill forts; the best and well worth seeing overlooks Aberystwyth at Pen Dinas; another, Gaer Fawr accessible, though overgrown in the summer, lies above and alongside the lane leading from Llanafan village into the Ystwyth valley. But there are links with prehistory alive and more immediate seeming than these. The late Professor H. J. Fleure in his book, *The Natural History of Man*, deduces from skull measurements and facial characteristics that the long-headed moorland people of Plinlimon and north Cardiganshire of today are a relic population of the late Palaeolithic Age (say 10,000 B.C.). The coracle, still used for fishing the Teifi around Cenarth, is

Between Tregaron and Abergwesin.
Forestry Commission planting in progress (1970).
Lines of trees follow contours where possible
and look much better in the landscape
than when they were more regimented

The rocky coast:
p14 Near New Quay
p15 above Near Llangranog *below* Cwmtudu

a survival from before the Roman occupation.

Traces of the Roman north-to-south road, Sarn Helen, can be deduced from stretches of moorland roads and tracks, and nothing remains above ground of the only known Roman camp, Loventium, in Llanddewi Brefi parish. There are the remains of a Norman castle dating from the earliest phase of the Norman Conquest at Cardigan but little is left of the castle at Aberystwyth, associated with the Edwardian subjugation of north Wales in the 13th century. There are many 12th- or 13th-century Norman and Welsh castle mounds (marked *Castell* on the O.S. maps), of the motte and bailey type. A typical and accessible example is in Llandyssul parish, a mile north of Pontshaen.

There are legends, of course, of the Dark Ages. The best known, because it has been embroidered by Thomas Love Peacock, is of a lost Atlantis below the shores of Cardigan Bay, once protected from the sea by a great embankment, the care of which was entrusted to Seithenyn ap Seithenyn Sardi, one of Wales' greatest drunkards. Because of his neglect the sea broke through and drowned sixteen fortified towns of Gwaelod and the surrounding countryside. But the causeway to this lost land from the shore north of Aberystwyth now appears to be nothing but an accumulation of shingle.

The underlying rocks are Ordovician and Silurian shales, slate and grits, providing building material in the form of bluish grey slabs, seen in the older buildings in the county, and, less frequently, greenish coloured sandstone. Rich deposits of lead, copper and zinc had apparently been exhausted by the beginning of this century, or their exploitation had become uneconomic. The lead contained enough silver to warrant a mint at Aberystwyth and established great fortunes. Early in the 17th century Sir Thomas Myddelton spent his in bringing fresh water to the heart of London through the New River Cut from Amwell in Hertfordshire. Wits might say that he prepared the way for the influx

13

of Cardiganshire dairymen into the metropolis.

The upland climate is bleak, with an annual rainfall as high as 100 inches, but it is much milder along the coast under the shelter of the northern and eastern mountains. The coastal strip is narrow and from the road north of Cardigan the sea is rarely glimpsed, except around Aberaeron. The shore is mostly shingle but there are fine sands in the Teifi estuary, and in the north at Borth. Cliff scenery, while it cannot compare with the Pembrokeshire coast, is far from insignificant, especially between Cardigan and New Quay.

New Quay's gay terraces and its harbour over-look a lovely arc of Cardigan Bay, and make it the most beautiful of the coastal resorts; Aberaeron is interesting for its layout and late Regency architecture. The importance of Aberystwyth as a resort, which began early in the 19th century and was quickened by the railway link with England in 1864, tends now to be overshadowed by its cultural, political and administrative development. The interior towns owe nothing to alien influence. Developing from native settlements, generally at some convenient valley or river site, they are essentially Welsh in their hardly

LLANSAINTFFRAID. Lleyn Peninsular (Caernarvonshire) beyond

definable personality, compounded of sedate and eccentric architecture and adornment. Often and quite unjustly disdained in the past, they are sustained by the trade of the surrounding countryside, the Forestry Commission and an occasional woollen mill. Of the five thousand or so farms in the county, as many as two thousand have less than twenty acres, and two thousand have between twenty and one hundred acres. Where, out of the valleys, the soil is thin and leached by heavy rainfall, and where the cost of essential minerals increases with the distance from centres of production, only pride and an inbred spirit of independence sustain human effort. It is in these regions that the depopulation figures are frightening. Two-thirds of the young people of the county leave it before they reach the age of twenty-five, and Cardiganshire has twenty thousand people fewer than it had a

Hill farms:
p20 Near Ponterwyd
   Above Bont-rhyd-y-beddau
   Above Tal-y-bont
p21 Abergwesin Pass near Soar a Mynydd
   Below Nant y Moch

hundred years ago. The visitor sees little of this; the friendly-looking, whitewashed cottages and farms catch the eye; the roofless, abandoned buildings merge into the landscape. Although by English standards the farms are small and difficult, within Cardiganshire there has been made a great contribution towards changing for the better the state of agricultural land throughout Britain and beyond. Continuing Professor Stapledon's earlier success in improved strains of grasses, the Plant Breeding Station at Plâs Gogerddan near Aberystwyth, part of the University, is now perfecting breeding techniques which will revolutionise cereal, grass, and other

Farm groups: *opposite* Between Tregaron and Llanddewi Brefi   *below* Llangeitho

21

opposite Manor House, Abermad in the Ystwyth valley
above Hafod, before demolition
below Derelict Bronwydd

p24 above Cross Inn, Ffair-rhos, Pontrhydfendigaid
p24 below Llanddewi Brefi
p25 above near Blaenpennal
p25 below Llansaintffraid, Cross Inn

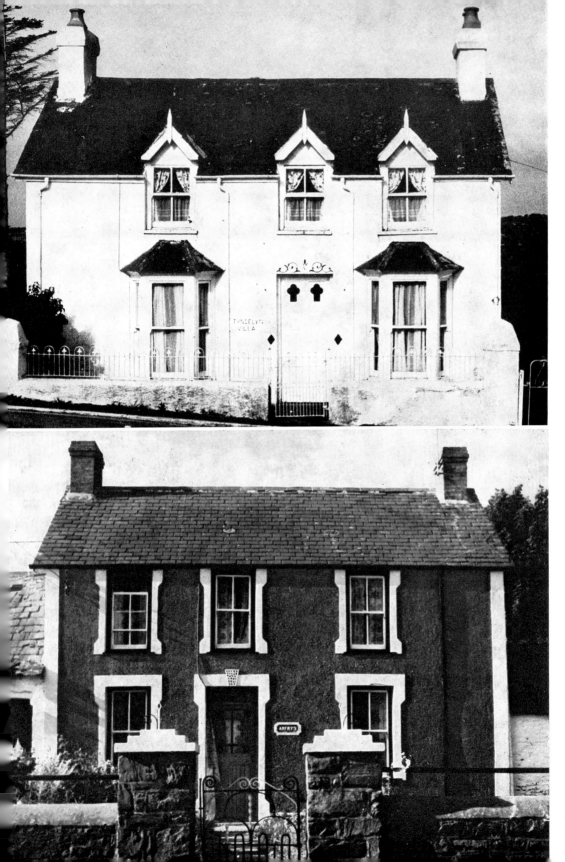

Llanon Methodist Chapel, LLANSAINTFFRAID

crop production and be worth millions of pounds in production of food.

There are no great houses on the English scale; but along the valleys there is an abundance of small country houses adorning the beauty of their natural settings. They mark the modest prosperity of a class that thrived before the mineral resources were exhausted, and road and rail transport killed the sea-borne trade. Mostly late Georgian in style, stonebuilt, stuccoed and painted under hipped slate roofs with well disposed windows, their like is described by Jane Austen and Trollope. Monachty in Llanbadarn Trefeglwys is a perfect example. Where darker stone has been left unplastered the effect is depressing. This is particularly noticeable at Nanteos, one of the well-proportioned early Georgian houses, in Llanbadarn y Creuddyn Lower (its Palladian stable screen is the best thing of its kind in the county). Llanayron House in Ciliau Aeron, less distinguished architecturally

and in a very similar setting is much more attractive with its pale pink coat. Most of the best houses in the county have gone, or have sunk into ruin; Hafod is a heap of rubble; C. R. Cockerell's Classical Derry Ormond is razed to the ground; Penson's romantically Rhenish Bronwydd is roofless and forlorn; Blaenpant is partly in ruins; and there are more.

There are no great medieval churches. There is a great sense of the past and of holiness in the cruciform church of Llanbadarn Fawr, but the average parish church, particularly in the eroding climate of the uplands, is more often than not a mid-Victorian re-building, slighted as "mean" in earlier guides and directories. R. J. Withers of Sherborne seems to have been the favourite architect or restorer. William Butterfield (see Llangorwen) has three churches in and around Aberystwyth. Penbryn, Mwnt (see

Bethesda, LLANDDEWI BREFI

26

Verwick) and Cellan are good examples of the primitive type of church lightly restored within a medieval fabric. Llanwenog has the best array of medieval features. Strata Florida, Llansantffraid (quite unspoilt) and Eglwys Fach have interesting early 19th-century and pre-Gothic-Revival interiors; Llangynllo and Llanafan are richly Victorian, and Ystrad Meurig better-than-average late Victorian. There are fragments of medieval (Flemish) glass in Cardigan (a parish church well worth visiting) and Llanfihangel y Creuddyn Upper, and a small glowing Victorian window at Lledrod Ucha. There is modern stained glass by Wilhelmina Geddes, Kenneth Baynes, John Hayward and Roy Lewis.

There are many early and mid-19th-century village chapels in the Classical or Gothic style, often very showy in adornment and colour contrasts. For town chapels Bethania (Cardigan) is hard to beat and it is rich in interior decoration and detail as well, spacious and imposing in the true Nonconformist preaching house tradition. Great religious revivals are associated with chapels in Llangeitho and Blaenannerch (Aberporth).

Sometimes the best building is the village school. Tremain on the coast road north of Cardigan is a sensible blend of modern design and traditional material, and at Cwmcoy in Brongwyn parish is good contemporary work. But the tourist's attention is centred more on the early- and mid-Victorian examples, usually Gothic in conception, with sharp gables and elaborate traceries in their pointed windows—"a Victorian compound of sense and sensibility" in Goodhart Rendel's phrase. Their interest is more than architectural. The county's influence in political, educational and other cultural movements in Wales and beyond has been out of all proportion to its sparse and materially underprivileged population. The village school can claim much of the credit.

Halfway between north and south Wales, the people of Cardiganshire, Welsh and Welsh-speaking to the core, have a closer affinity to the south in the subtlety of their intelligence and their spontaneity of expression and friendliness; even to one who is not a complete stranger to Wales, there is a particular, inescapable feeling of foreignness in this outpost of a lovely land, sensed in the character of such places as Aberaeron and Tregaron, and in the Saturday market of Cardigan; even in the wayside cemeteries and their elaborate memorials. It is clear that the western seaboard culture of Europe has left some trace of its passage in other than megaliths and dolmens.

Cardiganshire: Gazetteer

The number after each entry refers to the square on the map of Cardiganshire where the place is to be found

Aberaeron (5). Where the hills gently fold back from the coast to leave a narrow plain, the river Aeron forms at its mouth a small natural harbour which was shaped early in the 19th century from a fishing hamlet into a trading port; as such, it prospered for fifty years or so until the railway from Shrewsbury to Aberystwyth gradually diminished the seaborne traffic. Geometrical in pattern as far as the lie of the land permits, it survives like Milford, Pembroke Dock and Portmadoc as a period piece of Regency architecture and planning, modest enough but thoughtfully coherent. Its central buildings, copy-book Classical in style, with plain well composed fronts, are a welcome change from the gables, bay windows and silvered railings of other Welsh seaside towns. Perhaps the prevalent exuberance of colour wash—seen at its best when in softly contrasting shades of grey and white—marks a native reaction from classical formalism towards non-conformity. A special feature is the decoration of quoins and window mouldings. Street names provide clues to the stages of development: Waterloo, Wellington, Regent, Victoria, Albert.

The early development was largely sponsored by a squarson, Alban Gwynne of Tyglyn in Llanddewi Aberarth parish (*q.v.*), and there is no evidence for the local assertion that John Nash had a hand in it. It provided jetties, quays, stores, an imposing harbour-master's house, now a hotel, an elegant Classical style Town Hall and an inner and outer harbour. The area of the inner harbour became the town centre; chestnut trees grow at the quayside bordered by Regency houses. As so often along this coast the atmosphere is Continental; Brittany is suggested. Although the shore is an exposed shingle bank few seaside places in Wales are as charming as this. A large bare caravan site in the northern outskirts is set sufficiently apart.

Holy Trinity Church, largely of 1887 by Prothero and Phillpot, with its low tower of light and dark stone, looks suburban and incongruous. The interior is heavy with stained glass. The triptych reredos is sumptuous.

Housing development inland through the Aeron valley from Alban Square is pleasantly circumspect, and often quite charming in architectural detail.

Aberporth (7). Once a quiet seaside village, its old cottages and oriel-windowed Victorian villas are almost completely obscured by modern housing development, with a jazzy village school. The Ministry of Technology Establishment fences, radar screens, KEEP OUT notices, etc., are inescapable. But the beach is good and visitors flock to it. The Church of St Cynfil, at the southern entrance to the village, was built in 1856 (architect R. J. Withers).

The gaunt Calvinistic Methodist chapel at *Blaenannerch*, a straggling village on the main coast road, has outwardly little to commend it, but it saw the start of the last religious revival in Wales in living memory, that of 1904, when three evangelical preachers, Seth Joshua, Joseph Jenkins and Evan Roberts attended a conference there and, through prayer, the latter particularly, were inspired and compelled to missionary work through all Wales, with an immediate though not so profound effect on its social structure and way of life. Dr Eifion Evans (*The Welsh Revival of 1904*) writes of the revival: "its effects were so evidently supernatural, its fruits so patently holy, that none could reasonably doubt its divine source".

Aberystwyth (2). Settled life began here about 600 B.C. within the Iron Age fort of *Pen Dinas* 400 feet sheer above a natural harbour and flanked by the Rheidol and Ystwyth rivers.

Shaped like an hour glass and now partly under cultivation, its ramparts can be clearly traced and the site is dominated by an uncompleted 19th-century column like a factory chimney, put up by a local squire, Major Richardes of Brynyreithen, in honour of the Duke of Wellington. In the 6th century St Padarn founded a monastery a mile or so inland on the plain below, where Llanbadarn church now stands. Civil administration began towards the end of the 13th century under the shelter of a stone castle built at the water's edge on the order of Edward I. The harbour area grew into a busy seaport following the exploitation of the county's rich mineral resources. High Street was laid out in the 18th century and a small square of Georgian houses, now Laura Place; a few of the houses with elegant fanlights and fronts remain on its north side, and on the east side the old Assembly Rooms, designed by George S. Repton in 1820, are now the headquarters of the University Students Union.

In 1788 the rich Herefordshire squire, Uvedale Price of Foxley, a close friend of Colonel Johnes of Hafod, acquired a piece of waste ground near the castle, then a romantic ruin. On it John Nash (see Introduction) designed a summer house for Lady Price. Old prints show it to have been a triangular fortress-type building with an octagonal tower at each corner and, on the seaward elevation, a single-storey bow providing a balcony for an upstairs drawing room. This eccentric building, known as the Castle House, was later swallowed up in the University building, but a model of it in Worcester china has been preserved.

The town now began to attract visitors, lured by the romantic scenery inland and the salubrious air of the coast. Victorian developers were close behind and the town expanded northward, along and behind the crescent of the bay. The big

ABERAERON

time of expansion came in 1864 when the railway was extended from Shrewsbury, with two trains a day to and from London. The terminus, with access to the promenade along a gridiron of streets, drew shopping interests away from the cramped lanes of the earlier quarter. The town is almost entirely mid- to late-Victorian and a sweep of tall, gabled bay-windowed boarding houses fronts the shingle beach from the pierhead to the foot of 500 feet high *Constitution Hill* on the northern edge. The latter, with *Pen Dinas* at the other end, effectively blocks any coast line sprawl which is often such a depressing feature of coast resorts. Occasionally an earlier villa survives among the inland terraces, notably *Sandmarsh Cottage*, double bowed from wide eaves to the ground level at the lower end of Queen's Road.

Churches and chapels abound, mostly late 19th- and early 20th-century. The *Roman Catholic church*

of St Winifred in Queen's Road was designed by a local architect George Jones and built in 1875. The *parish church* of St Michael and All Angels designed by Nicholson and Sons, Hereford, and built in 1890 of York-shire stone with a western tower added in 1906, is on the south side of Laura Place; its large grassy churchyard backs on to the castle mound. It has conventional Kempe style stained glass in the five-light east window and pleasant 1962 glass in purple, russet brown and green of St Cecilia and St Francis in the north aisle. The elaborate reredos of Ancaster stone reproduces Leonardo da Vinci's *Last Supper*. Off Trinity Road *Holy Trinity church* was built in 1886, and enlarged by tower and transepts in 1888 of local stone with Bath stone dressings, to the design of Middleton and Son, Westminster. The interior walls are unplastered and the floor is of wood blocks. Its elaborate reredos of gilt figures

depicts the Annunciation, the Adora-tion and the Death of Christ. It is flanked by angels and topped by a tall crocketed finial. Above it a five-light window glows with closely wrought stained glass, mainly blues and reds. There is a splendid brass lectern. *St Mary's* Welsh church in Bath Road, a chapel of ease to the parish church and by comparison a modest affair, is the smaller of the three churches in the county designed by William Butterfield and was built in 1866. It is of local dark stone with Bath dressings and pent house aisles and has little to suggest the work of the master.

Nonconformist architecture is mainly mid-Victorian and later, less exuberant than many of the earlier chapels in the south of the county; the most striking is *Seilo* Welsh Presbyterian at the junction of Northgate Street and Queen's Road. Despite the modern doors and fittings, long plate glass windows

and grey mosaic work, the entrance elevation of long square pillars up to a slatted pediment, topped by a small belfry, has something of the earlier Classical tradition and is faintly reminiscent of New England. In New Street a tiny *Unitarian Meeting House* with almost miniature round windows above the double doors is pre- or early-Victorian, and nearby is *Elim Four Square Gospel church*.

Of the 20th century: the War Memorial in the Castle grounds, a bronze figure of Victory by the Italian sculptor Routelli, and, inland, on higher ground to the east, the *National Library of Wales* and the adjacent new University blocks. The library, an imposing square block faced with Cornish granite and Portland stone above a long flight of steps, was built in stages from 1911 (architect Sidney Kyffin Greenslade), on land presented by Lord Rendel. Organised into three main groups, Printed Books, Manuscripts and Records, and Prints, Maps and Drawings, it houses a collection of Celtic, English and foreign medieval and modern literature and manuscripts as well as records and papers of landed families. On a nearby 450-acre site the new buildings of the University College, designed by Sir Percy Thomas & Son and others, mark the shift of cultural emphasis from the sea front to the hill.

Historically and architecturally the most interesting building is the first *University College* on the sea front. In 1864 a partnership between David Davies, founder of the Llandinam family, and an English contractor Thomas Savin had pushed the railway to the coast. Savin had visions of a great tourist industry from Towyn in Merioneth to Aberystwyth. He bought Castle House, then much dilapidated, and instructed J. P. Seddon to plan its enlargement into a hotel on a grand scale. The day he received his instructions Seddon sketched on the spot a plan for the south wing and immediately Savin engaged workmen to start on the foundations, sending Seddon back to London to prepare more drawings. The work proceeded at a frantic pace, often in advance

ABERYSTWYTH. The war memorial

of the finished drawings, which in their completed form envisaged a fantastic structure along the sea wall, a mixture of Early English, Perpendicular and Tudor half timbering, all richly embellished under roofs of different levels capped by pinnacles, castellated towers and turrets. Within little more than a year, after spending £80,000, Savin, caught in a credit squeeze when Bank Rate rose to 10 per cent and tourists did not arrive, was forced into bankruptcy. Eventually the hotel, unfinished, was bought for £10,000 by a group of Welshmen anxious to found a Welsh non-denominational university. Seddon was again called in to adapt the hotel to its new purpose; his design was even more fantastic, as wildly romantic as the crags and peaks of the mountains beyond. Had it been completed, it would have been one of the great monuments to Victorian architecture in Britain. In 1885, with the building far from completion, fire destroyed the greater part of the interior but the southern wing was saved and

remains today. Seddon's work can also be seen in the façade of the northern wing; the four-storey library block was built in the mid-1890s to the design of C. J. Ferguson, and replaced Nash's Castle House.

While Seddon was busy at the College, another London architect, C. J. Hayward, was engaged on the *Queens Hotel* towards the northern end of the sea front, now a County Council establishment. Gothic in style, faced with local stone, it is soft purple in colour and relieved with freestone dressings. Later, Seddon was commissioned to design a terrace immediately beyond the hotel, now *Victoria Terrace*. The first two houses were completed to his design, each one of five storeys and basement. He set out to introduce a richer colouring than the drab washes of most of the sea front houses, choosing red brick for ground work with a mixture of buff and blue Staffordshire bricks above. The columns forming the window mullions were of delicately coloured sandstone. The corner house—the

Forestry Commission office—is now painted in the colour which Seddon sought to avoid, and his detail is obscured, although it is still visible on his other house. Beyond again, the terrace from Blaenllynant to Alexandra Hall is the most coherent row along the front.

Aberystwyth is the administrative centre of the county; a link between north and south Wales through the Welsh National Library, and through the University College a cultural centre of rapidly expanding importance. It is a mainly Victorian or early Edwardian period piece, as architecture, with the 20th century well in the background; a watering place with a reputation as a Welsh Torquay for spring and winter convalescence. In the summer it is a magnet for day trips for Sunday School and Senior Citizens from hinterland villages. Resident visitors

ABERYSTWYTH
right The first University College
below left and right
Terraces on the front

Llyn Fanod, BLAENPENNAL

abound. The Borough Council's guide is excellent.

Bettws Bledrws *see* **Llangybi.**

Bettws Ifan (7). A small inland parish, falling steeply on its east side into the Ceri valley. West of St John's Church (rebuilt 1870), an avenue of beech trees leads to *Glan Medeni*, a small, two-storeyed early 19th-century country house, typical of the district. Nearby *Watch Tower* chapel, 1865, is built of stone in the earlier Classical tradition with round-headed windows on its gabled front and square windows at the side. The interior is in its original state with low box pews. *Troedyraur House*, seen across the valley from the Beulah/Brongest road is a series of four blocks, irregular in proportion and elevation, all late Georgian, with a verandah on the east end and cobbled approach on the north. Now a farm house, its interior has been largely remodelled but the principal room retains Ionic columns, mahogany doors and gilt decorated pelmets. Fine oak trees and rhododendrons adorn the grounds.

Bettws Leucu (5). A watery parish, thinly populated, on the south flank of the upper Aeron valley. A cottage or two and a Marley village hall adjoin the featureless 1875 church of St Michael near the river bank.

Blaenpennal (5). Is in a landscape of desolate, natural beauty where rough pasture mingles with marsh and heather, and abandoned roofless buildings signify the end of human endeavour. The church of St David rebuilt in 1903 is a plain unadorned single chamber. *Llyn Fanod* is a small lake fringed with rushes and half ringed by treacherous swamps. Lichened boulders and small clusters of alder trees break the terrain, and nothing breaks the silence. Four parishes meet at a high point near it. *Sarn Helen*, the Roman road, is nearby too.

Borth (2). The long single-street village is built on a storm beach raised above the marsh land through which the Leri river reaches the Dovey Estuary. The backs of the houses and hotels which front the

sea impart a drabness to the street which, except for the 1842 village school with pretty Gothic windows, is almost entirely mid-Victorian and later. There are sand dunes at the northern end of the long sea front at *Ynys Las* opposite Aberdovey; at the southern end cliffs rise sheer above the sea and from the high ground on the road to Llangorwen (Clarach) there are fine views of Merioneth. There is considerable caravan development at each end. Stumps of an ancient forest visible at low tide mark the edge of a forest swamp lying below the peat of Borth Bog (*see* Llancynfelin).

Unlike many other such places Borth is not deserted out of season, and a strong village community exists. In summer the four miles of yellow sands from Ynys Las to the cliffs and at low tide far into the bay are ideal for children. In 1876, a serious epidemic closed Uppingham School for several years, and the boys and staff moved to Borth, attracted by its open position on Cardigan Bay and its invigorating air. They settled in a large four-square hotel

with a faint suggestion of Cheltenham—then the Cambrian and now renamed *Pantyfedwen*, a hostel for the University College, Aberystwyth. Parents visiting the school and their succeeding generations established an English influence and an 18-hole golf course along the shore towards the dunes.

The 1872 *parish church* of St Matthew rises on a mound to the west of the village across the railway line and on weekdays is best approached through Ynysfergi farm. Typical of its period, with nothing of antiquity, it has stained glass by Whitefriars, Celtic Studios and Shrigley and Hunt, Lancaster. Oak choir stalls and pulpit are good and the whole is well tended. So is the churchyard, under the shade of pine trees.

Brongwyn (7). Tiny parish with modern development including well designed village school at *Cwmcoy*, where, below late Georgian *Aberceri House*, the Ceri river joins the swirling Teifi. *St Mary's Church* in the lanes north of Cwmcoy is a simple singlechamber building remote among cypress, Irish yew, pine and chestnut trees, with stabling nearby. The fabric is medieval. 19th-century pointed windows; white plastered interior walls. Plain oval tablet to Thomas Jones, Newcastle, and early 18thcentury tombstones.

Capel Bangor *see* **Melindwr.**

Cardigan (7). In architecture and personality a proper Welsh country town. At its southern and most interesting entrance a bank rises steeply from the medieval stone bridge with cutwaters and pedestrian recesses on the upstream side. Walls of a Norman castle, rebuilt and enlarged by Gilbert Marshall in 1240, come almost to the edge of the Teifi. Upstream, the Benedictine Priory group, now the parish church and the local hospital, is on the river bank, prompting thoughts of rich monastic harvests of salmon and sewin. Downstream, below St Dogmaels, the river opens to the estuary, and on its left bank high sycamore trees lap their lower branches in the water at high tide; opposite, part of the old quay has been converted with conscious municipal pride into a terrace of square paving stones, potted plants, seats and miniature cannons, and it is now hard to believe that the town was one of the principal western seaports, until the river silted up, and the railway, now closed, came in 1888. Development has been mainly northward up the long High Street, and, except for St Mary Street leading down to the church, is almost entirely 19thcentury. The only Georgian architecture of any note is the *Shire Hall*, now a furniture showroom, at the southern end of the High Street, and a block of offices on the northern side of St Mary Street. The courtroom of the upper storey of the Shire Hall is octagonal and domed at its west end, where the dock and witness box used to be and has Doric columns and good sash windows. The offices in St Mary Street built of courses of Cilgerran slate have a good frontage of four sash windows on each of the two storeys, underneath a pediment containing a half round window.

The dominant building is the

35

Guildhall, built in 1859 with a clock tower and turret added in 1892. Its main features are a high sloping roof, and the ponderous uniformity of slabs of Cilgerran slate above the low arches of slate and Bath stone with a capping of red bricks. As well as council offices, it houses a covered produce market with stalls grouped around a central quadrangle of arches, similar to those on the outside. The market is so popular that it has now spread to the basement where there is a similar layout of arches. The whole has a Breton, or even southern French atmosphere, and comes to life on the Saturday market day. The Welsh penchant for inventive adornment is seen in the four female heads of painted cast iron from a local foundry, fixed in the wall of the front elevation. On the steps outside is a Russian cannon from the Crimean War, trained on Priory Street and, around, a bewildering array of traffic signs.

St Mary's Church, in a churchyard where the rearrangement of tombstones gives a parade-ground look, was entirely rebuilt, except for the 14th-century chancel, from 1702 onwards. It has had fairly recent attention, and its interior is spacious and uncluttered. The chancel is impressive; it has a stone block floor and 20th-century stained glass (by Walter Wilkinson), with pieces of the original medieval Flemish glass (the rest was removed to Hafod) in the upper panes of the east window. The octagonal font is 15th-century, of light coloured stone. The *Priory*, adjacent to the church was rebuilt in 1802, reputedly to designs by John Nash; it has since been so altered for use as a hospital that its earlier character has gone but on the west front are the original Gothic pointed windows with elaborately interlaced bars. Katherine Phillips, the poet, Orinda to her friends (b. 1631, d. 1664) lived here as wife of the High Sheriff.

There are many chapels; the best is 1847 *Bethania* in early 19th-century William Street. It has a wide-eaved gable front, and a portico with Doric Columns and pediment. Its interior is even better, with original low box

CARDIGAN Market Hall, the basement

pews and gallery to seat nine hundred, an elaborate pulpit, and it shows good craftsmanship in the ceiling mouldings and cornices. A less stern-looking chapel is the pink-washed *Tabernacle* in High Street. Dated 1760, it has had a 1902 refacing in pretty Gothic.

The gaol, designed by John Nash in 1793, was finally demolished in the early 1890s to make way for Bingham Terrace, opposite the junction of High and Napier Streets. *Stanley House*, well proportioned in an early Victorian style, is on the site of the gaoler's house, and at its back, small blocked-in circular windows in the solid stone masonry suggest that Nash's work may not have disappeared completely. Parallel to and west of High Street, a silent lane of crumbling cottages and sheds leading to the quay is haunted by ghosts of bygone mariners. There is a council estate at *Maesglas* and chic, gardened

villas on the Gwbert road in many styles, including Dutch.

As a background to the exuberance and bustle of the High Street the architecture of the town may be subdued, but it is interesting in its variety and decoration; not without occasional eccentricity, even waywardness, as in the 1935 *Court House* in Priory Street.

Caron Is Clawd *see* **Tregaron.**

Caron Uwch Clawd *see* **Pontrhyd-fendigaid.**

Cellan (8). The valley road running east from the outskirts of Lampeter is bordered by high hedges which restrict the view, while to the south lanes lead steeply through bracken and pasture to the high moors of the Carmarthenshire boundary, and on to the Roman Road, at over a thousand feet. Here the land is

CARDIGAN bridge

37

boulder-strewn and desolate and at the roadside the walls of abandoned cottages give shelter to sheep, and shade for summer picnics. The northward views are immense in their sweep, and from the ridge of higher ground to the south into the far distance the crests of the Carmarthenshire ranges are outlined like waves. On the southern boundary of the parish *Bryn Hirfaen* rises to twelve hundred feet. On its reverse slope the monolith which gives the hill its name is in the next county.

The valley church of St Cellan is simple and primitive. Its walls of rubble and rough boulders at and just above ground level give character. The porch is large with stone seats on either side, and medieval timber supports the roof. A low pointed arch leads to the simply restored interior which has plenty of light through clear glass in renewed lancets. There is painted floral work on the boarded ceiling, a reading desk on either side of the chancel arch, and no pulpit. The stoup and medieval font have been preserved. A pretty parish, of contrasts and character.

Ceulany Maes Mawr (3). Beautiful landscapes. Valleys of the Leri and the Ceulan converge at Talybont, and the Clettwr, forming the northern boundary and meeting the main road, A.487, meets them at Tre'r ddol. The Leri forms a deep ravine, thickly wooded and overlooked by the road leading to Elerch village. The Ceulan valley is wider, and, as it is not so thickly wooded, the views are more sweeping. It is overlooked on its southern flank by the Mountain Road from Talybont, well surfaced all the way, over the Nant y Moch reservoir dam to Pont Erwyd on the main Aberystwyth to Rhayadr road. But it is narrow, and when it emerges from the tree line (if you are lucky you may see a kite) the valley side is precipitous and unfenced. Near its highest point an unmade loosely surfaced track, liable to subsidence, leads off to the left near old lead mine workings to drop down to a group of four small lakes and the *Angler's Retreat,* a private bungalow and not a fishing inn, the only sign of habitation in this desolate, stone scored landscape where

deep ploughing suggests preparation for forestry plantations. Past the Angler's Retreat the track peters out north of Llyn Penrhaiadr.

The Clettwr valley too can be reached from Talybont past Taliesin's reputed grave (*Bedd Taliesin*), a flat stone like the capstone of a dolmen on the mountainside beyond a north fork of the Mountain Road. Taliesin, a 6th century A.D. bard, some of whose poems in Old Welsh are preserved in the National Library, Aberystwyth, was found as a child in a salmon trap on the Dovey (Thomas Love Peacock's *Misfortunes of Elphin*).

Talybont then is the gateway to this splendid scenery, a fair sized village on the main coast road, once important for its woollen mills and lead mining. The Lerry woollen mill alone survives, and visitors come to see its products and the hand-loom weaving machinery still in use since its installation in 1809. Two small hotels in close proximity—*the Black and the White Lion*—overlook the village centre. The Black Lion has a pretty front of grey dressed stone, and round headed arches above the well spaced windows. Fronting the main street, *Bethel* chapel stands up well behind painted railings and clipped Irish yews. It has two gabled porches and four pointed tracery windows. The Victorian lamp-post is worth a glance. The 1909 *parish church* of St David on the northern outskirts of the village is rather ugly, in contrasting dark rusticated and lighter coloured free stone. The 1959 stained glass in the small three-light window at the east end is by Kenneth Baynes, of rich deep colour; influenced by Rouault, it portrays The Good Shepherd under crossed crooks and has a Welsh inscription *Myfi Yw Y Bugail Da (I am the Good Shepherd).*

Elerch on the southern boundary of the parish has a church (St Peter's) designed by William Butterfield built in 1868. It was originally a daughter church of Llangorwen (see latter for association with the Oxford Movement). Gregorian plainsong is still chanted at services; the men sit apart from the women and approach the altar first at Holy Communion. It is a simple stone building of nave, chancel and two transepts. The low

tower, slate roofed, rising above the chancel gives it rather an alien look in this upland village. The interior is entirely Victorian, and the chancel arch is picked out in chocolate and red colour—which Butterfield might not have found amiss.

Cilcennin (5). A village of scattered smallholdings and new houses around a nucleus formed by the good-looking Commercial Inn and the church of The Holy Trinity. This has a bellcote and is by A. Ritchie, 1888, with elaborate tombstones and memorials in the modern Welsh idiom. There is a village centre west of the church, around the handsome school and 1859 Congregational chapel *Sion,* the best building in the village, white with two central windows duplicated by smaller ones to light the gallery, and double, grained doors all under chocolate-coloured arches. Grey and green washed cottages adjoining the Commercial Inn make a good group, and due east a beech fringed lane, signposted *Bethania* and *Penuwch,* runs to bleak moorland and recent forestry plantations, past lonely, substantial farmsteads.

Ciliau Aeron (5). Along the eastern boundary of the parish, A.482, keeping company with a single track railway and the river Aeron, shows at every one of its gentle curves a still more entrancing prospect of steep wooded banks and overhanging trees. The roadside cottages have the smug, family-retainer air of their early Victorian origin, with pointed latticed windows and an occasional low verandah. Here in the northern tip of the parish and at a point where the main road touches shoulders with the railway there is an open view across parkland and against a hanger of massed oaks, of pink washed, two-storey *Llanayron House,* almost in its original late Georgian condition. It has a good west elevation of five sash windows on each storey, the lower under round-headed arches. In his 1795 *Guide through Wales,* James Baker names John Nash as the architect. A minor road runs at the back of the house past its courtyard, site of an earlier house, and a small, free standing, lodge-like building with a pediment porch and a square lantern. It was once the billiard room. In the

Cardiganshire country. Fields and hedgerow trees near LAMPETER

park is *Llanerch Aeron Church of St Non,* a nave and chancel building of 1798 with a low west tower, pinnacled at each corner and capped by a low cupola. Meyrick's *History and Antiquities of Cardiganshire* illustrates it as having stuccoed walls with low battlemented parapets. It is tempting, at least, to suggest that John Nash was responsible for the inspiration of these buildings. At any rate they are built very much in his spirit. In 1878, the church was savagely mauled, probably by F. Fowler of Brecon. The stucco was removed; so were the parapets and blue and yellow tinted glass was inserted in the lattice windows.

Westward, a secondary road towards Dihewid climbs sharply to five hundred feet above the valley bed. The parish church of St Michael lies on this road, a simple single chamber rebuilt in 1872 on its original site, as ancient yews and an almost circular

churchyard testify. This, with an adjacent farm and a few cottages, comprises the village.

Clarach *see* **Llangorwen.**

Cwmrheidol (3). A.4120 from Pont Erwyd to Devil's Bridge skirts the eastern edge of the wooded Rheidol ravine past the bellcoted church of 1827 (St John the Baptist) at *Yspytty Cynfyn.* Among cypress, yew and monkey puzzle trees and enclosed by a stone wall in which five large boulders, one standing about eleven feet above the ground, attest a prehistoric site. The surface of many of the graves is pebbled and some have crosses picked out in white quartz. The interior of the church is simple and beautifully kept. It has white plastered walls, tinted glass in the pointed windows and the Commandments, Creed and Lord's Prayer finely written in Welsh in gold lettering on

a black background and dated 1836; a curious small wooden font, probably late 19th-century, has an octagonal bowl on which scriptural scenes are carved in high relief, supported by eight male and female caryatids. The stained glass in the three-light east window is by Celtic Studios. Over the hill past the churchyard a footpath winds down to *Parsons Bridge,* an iron structure deep in the Rheidol ravine: well-known beauty spot.

Pont Erwyd is a sizeable wayside village where the George Borrow Hotel is a good stopping place on the road between Aberystwyth and Llangurig. Near it a lane leads to the almost deserted mining hamlet of *Ystumtuen* where the village school is now a Youth Hostel. There are spectacular views from the hill leading down to it. At the east end of Pont Erwyd a good mountain road to Talybont passes Nant y Moch reservoir (*see* Melindwr). On the way, a ruined cottage, *Aber Ceiro Fach,* on the left of the road is the birthplace of Sir John Rhys (1840–1915), philologist and first Celtic Professor at Oxford University. One route to the highest point of Plinlimon Fawr is from *Eisteddfa Gurig,* a little over four miles northeast of Ponterwyd on A.44.

Devil's Bridge *see* **Llanfihangel y Creuddyn Upper.**

Dihewid (8). There are fine valley views on the way here from Llanfihangel Ystrad. The crossroads village is rather grim with council house development. The single chambered church (St Vitalis) is neat inside with whitewashed walls and pale green plastered ceiling. Rebuilt about 1820. Next door a former school house and stable, dated 1855. Monkey puzzle tree and cedar. The Congregational chapel of 1861 at *Troedyrhiw* is well proportioned, with round-headed clear glass windows in front, square at back. Twin doors have elegant fanlights, and transoms. Inside colour scheme is green and mauve walls, with pink boarded ceiling and pink window embrasures; very showy.

Eglwys Fach *see* **Ysgubor y Coed.**

Gartheli (8). A hillside parish of small fields and streams with a small settlement at *Llwyn y groes* from which a good road runs due west. Off it, the parish church of St Gartheli, rebuilt in 1871, is sad and lonely with no vestige of antiquity. *Abermeurig Hall* at the western end is a pleasant 18th-century small country house of three storeys with a fine range of outbuildings, facing the parkland of the Meurig valley and bright with flowers.

Geneu yr Glyn *see* **Llandre.**

Gwbert *see* **Cardigan.**

Gwnnws Issa *see* **Ystrad Meurig.**

Gwnnws Ucha *see* **Pontrhydfendigaid.**

Gwynfil (5). A tiny civil parish with its northern boundary touching Llangeitho; otherwise nothing but a few scattered farms, no church, chapel or

post office. From the high ground above Llangeitho and through the hedges on the B.4343 road is an Arcadian view down the Aeron valley of green hills over the darker green of the spreading and richly wooded plain.

Henfynyw Upper (5). Traditionally, St David spent his boyhood here; the name is a corruption of Hên (or old) Menevia, the latter being the name given by the Romans to the St Davids district of Pembrokeshire. This is a small mainly coastal parish where the cliffs recede and the green hills drop gently to the plain at Aberaeron. Between the coast road and the cliffs the land is bare, with a feeling of aridity and space. At *Ffosyfin* on the coast road a lychgate with wooden Calvary and cobbled floor gives on to an avenue of pine trees that leads to R. J. Withers' simple 1864 church of St David.

Lampeter (8). The elaborate pattern of thousands of cribbed, rectangular fields with dark lines or hedges gives a special character to the countryside. They pattern the slopes of the several valleys that converge here in the Teifi basin and create an Arcadian setting to this small market town. In the centre the wide main street, dog-leg in shape, is bordered by a variety of shops under local, not chain, name-plates, and an occasional private house, grey fronted and anonymous behind opaquely curtained sash windows. Two handsome hotels with Georgian façades break the street frontage on either side, and weight is imparted by the 1888 *Town Hall,* civic in brick, Bath stone and green paint. This opens into the cattle market, and houses a Court Room where the County Assize used to be held; the whole block replaces one built to the design of P. F. Robinson. Terraced houses line the lanes that open from the main street. A friendly place and very Welsh, especially on market day (Tuesday).

The parish church of St Peter on a hillside overlooking the town was rebuilt in 1869 (R. J. Withers, architect). 17th century and later memorials from the previous church hang in the porch. The building is high and sombre, of dark stone with a

short spire rising from the tower in the southwest corner. It does little justice to its fine position. There is subdued stained glass by Whitefriars and R. J. Newberry in the Victorian interior. The Brangwynesque Expressionist stained glass in the large west window, 1938, is of Christ, Peter and Andrew. Designed by Wilhelmina Geddes, it is to a member of the Harford family, benefactors of the town, of Blaise Castle, Bristol and Falcondale on the north outskirts of the parish.

Near St Peters, the Roman Catholic church of Our Lady of Mount Carmel is a modern building, cream coloured inside with grey brick arches and apse walls. The inscriptions, including those of the Stations of the Cross, are in Welsh. Chapel architecture is subdued late Victorian. The earliest chapel, once Baptist, is now a builder's yard behind the Eagle Stores.

Lampeter is well known in Wales for *St Davids University College,* founded in 1822 by Thomas Burgess, Bishop of St Davids and son of a grocer in Odiham, Hants. His object was to provide education of a University standard, in the hope that it would attract young men to the service of the Church in the diocese; contrary to popular belief, it has never been solely a theological college. Bishop Burgess and many of his clergy and laity gave a tenth of their annual income to the endowment fund. King George IV contributed £1,000 from the Privy Purse and the City of Liverpool £6,000. C. R. Cockerell, then engaged on Derry Ormond House in the next parish of Llangybi, designed the main block, now the Old Building; in Goodhart Rendell's phrase "he stooped to Tudor", trimming his design to suit the College purse. The finished building found some favour in the eyes of Sir Gilbert Scott who, after a visit in 1848, wrote of it in a letter to the Principal as "a most charming example of the early Gothic revival showing a fine sense of scale and grouping, and even the faults of detail inherent in a revival of a strange style possess a naiveté which is not without attraction". Cockerell's design (his drawings are filed in the Bursar's office) was a low stuccoed quadrangle enclosing a central court from which staircases led

Slate engraving in LAMPETER churchyard

to student and common rooms; with a small tower, cupola capped, at each corner, and a square tower over a perpendicular arched south gateway (the statue of St David in the centre niche is the 1952 work of Mr Lindsay Clark). The north side included a library in the centre flanked by the chapel and hall, the façade having a cloister of eight bays, now unfortunately glassed in. Though the building was enlarged from 1880 onwards mainly by additions in the Tudor style on the north side, it is still very much as Cockerell left it. The chapel was rebuilt about 1880 in an earlier Gothic style, and renovated under the supervision of Sir T. G. Jackson, whose interior design was exhibited in the 1879 Royal Academy. The stalls, painted green with gold leaf ornament against maroon panels, came from New College Oxford and a panelled painted roof replaced the origina whitewashed roof. The carved reredos, designed by W. D. Caröe in the 1930s, is hardly in keeping with the rest of the interior. Caröe's wish that it should be painted was unfortunately not granted. The centre figure is the Good Shepherd with St David on one side and St Deinol on the other. The two paintings in the chapel are copies (Coreggio and Annibaele Caracci).

The college library, now housed in

LAMPETER. West window by Wilhelmina Geddes (1938)

the modern buildings, contains a large bequest by the famous collector, Thomas Phillips, of medieval manuscripts, incunabula and first editions. The oldest of the incunabula is a Latin translation of Plutarch, printed in Rome in 1470. There is an attractive David Cox drawing of the college in the Senior Common Room.

Fortunately no further extensions mar the charm and symmetry of Cockerell's work, which shows to advantage compared with the nearby Canterbury Building, now due for demolition, in dark rusticated stone by Professor Middleton of Cambridge, opened in 1886. Modern buildings are by Elidir Davies of London and even more recent ones by Alex Gordon and Partners. The

interior of the library is impressive. The College is residential and, under Royal Charters of 1852 and 1865, it has authority to confer B.A. and B.D. degrees. It had a difficult struggle for survival since the Treasury withdrew financial aid in 1874. Since 1961 it has had full financial aid from the University Grants Committee and is now a Constituent Institution of the University of Wales. Development plans envisage by 1973 a College devoted to the Arts and Humanities with about four hundred and fifty undergraduates. Women were admitted in 1966. It is a University in miniature, unique and remote in its pastoral setting.

The rural parish lies east of the town. There is a small forlorn Vic-

torian church, dedicated to St Mary, on the crossroads at *Maestir* whence a shady byroad runs to the *Fish and Anchor Inn*.

Falcondale, built in 1859 in Italianate style of cement-rendered brick, has three-storey wings with Venetian windows and a central two-storey block, all under wide eaves. It looks very well from the main road and is now an old people's home.

Llanafan (6). The mansion of *Trawscoed* or *Crosswood* is on the site of an earlier house sacked in 1645 by the Parliamentary forces under Sir William Middleton. The earlier rebuilding which appears to date from the early to middle 19th century is in two storeys; the crest and motto of the Lisburne family, still prominent landowners hereabouts, is in red relief under the cornices of the central pediment above an Ionic portico. The outward appearance of the whole has not been improved by the addition in 1891 of a vast, incongruous northern wing. The elaborately decorated library room, even now a museum piece, adapts 18th century notions to late Victorian taste. From the French windows of the library there is a view of an avenue of tall conifers, mainly cupressus in variety, with splendidly grown monkey puzzle trees. The house and grounds, taken over in 1946 by the Ministry of Agriculture and Fisheries as the headquarters of the *National Agricultural Advisory Service,* befit their beautiful setting in the tall, varied woodland of the Ystwyth valley.

The village is one of scattered houses, a flimsy 1930 village hall, a solid stone-built 1875 village school, a church with a terrace of cottages on the hillside to the northeast, and on its southern outskirts a showy, gabled 1806 Methodist chapel with roundheaded tracery windows, white walls with chocolate pinkish long and short quoins, and 1930 double porch entrances.

Clipped yew hedges border the asphalt path to the door of St Avan's Church, rebuilt in 1860 on ancient foundations, and restored in 1925. Inside, one is dismayed by the darkness but in artificial light there is a sense of tenderness, imparted by the designs and quality of the stained glass from the 1870s onwards, mainly to members of the Lisburne family, and by the painting, hanging on the north wall, of the Virgin garlanded in fruit. The small south transept is filled with Lisburne pews, and Lisburne hatchments take the place of windows on the north and south walls of the chancel. Beyond the terraced cottages a lane forks. The right fork passes through the gloom of fir plantations to come refreshingly out on to open moorland past a sad, small, square chapel with no inscription. The left fork, skirting the brackeny flank of *Gaer Fawr* earthwork, drops into the Ystwyth valley among the silent lead mine workings at *Lletysynod*.

Llanarth (8). A large parish with a bottleneck opening to the sea cliffs north of Llwyncelyn. The village is built on each side of a deep ravine, spanned by a narrow bridge just off A.487. Its roadside houses are mainly early 19th century, dominated by the tall 15th-century tower of the parish church of St David, the rest of which, cut into the hillside, was largely rebuilt in 1872 by R. J. Withers; it is more spacious, especially in the chancel, than his usual work in the county. The nave has good windows, particularly five lancets on the north side with deeply sloping sills. Antiquity is present in a display of 1613 Bibles in Welsh and English, an 11th-century font whose four-sided basin tapers to a square base of four carved lions (the whole sadly distempered), and in the remains of a churchyard cross carved in high relief. The churchyard gates carry a War Memorial of two polished bronze shields.

Good secondary roads go south through *Mydroilyn* (hairpin bend, and 1890 corrugated-iron church of The Holy Trinity) and undulating country, barely glimpsed over banked hedges until the open moorland. Interesting row of single storey primitive cottages, still occupied, at *Oakford*. Nearby on the Llanarth road *Neuadd*, late 18th-century, built on to an earlier house, stands well in parkland of oak and chestnut trees. It carries a 17th-century stone inscription of texts in Welsh and English and, under a primitive medieval carved head, the arms of the Ken-

Trawscoed garden, LLANAFAN

singtons of Pembrokeshire, who once owned the estate. There are good 18th-century outbuildings. It is now a guest house. Possibly here lived the noblewoman who shut up the goat of Evan Thomas (1710–1770). It strayed too near Llanarth Hall, and inspired the following lines (*Penguin Book of Welsh Verse* translated into English):

O black-maned, horse-haired unworthy one

What did you do to the goat, your sister?

She'd your father's horns, your mother's beard—

Why did you falsely put her in prison?

More primitive cottages, mostly in ruins at *Capel Vicar*. *Plas y Wern,* where Henry VII slept on his way to Bosworth, can be seen from the road to Newquay; 17th-century, remodelled early in the 19th, it has panelled rooms, a fine staircase, a small minstrels' gallery in an upper room, and carved scallops above the entrance door.

Llanbadarn Fawr (2). The great church of St Padarn dominates this small parish, now a suburb of Aberystwyth. Here above the Rheidol valley St Padarn, whose influence lay mainly to the southeast of Plinlimon, founded a monastery in the 6th century, and the church as it now stands was built on the site early in the 13th century. Cruciform, with a solid central tower, it is big and impresses by its external plainness. The only decoration is in the rich mouldings and carving of the 15th-century southern doorway, now weatherworn. But if this external plainness causes no surprise, the extreme simplicity of the interior, devoid of any architectural detail earlier than J. P. Seddon's 1870 restoration, must come as a shock. Except at the east end, all windows are single lancet, well proportioned and deeply splayed, some arranged in groups of three. The piers and arches below the tower are quite bare of ornament. In spaciousness the interior is Benedictine, in simplicity Cistercian; and these two orders in succession ruled the living until the Dissolution.

The chancel contains tablets from the mid-17th century onwards, of surprising elegance and grandeur. They are mainly to the Gogerddan and Nanteos families. The earliest, on the north side of the east window, is of John Jones of Nanteos, who raised a Royalist regiment in the Civil Wars. There are works by Flaxman, his pupil E. H. Baily, R. Wynne and William Townesend. In the south transept is a granite pillar cross, richly ornamented, about nine feet high, and another about five feet high of local sandstone. Professor V. E. Nash-Williams dates these respectively to the 10th and 9th–11th century A.D. There is a strong, even awesome, atmosphere in this building; credit is due to Seddon who raised the roof to its original height and inserted the present ceilings, rebuilt the walls of the nave, south porch, and spire; raised the chancel floor and paved it with black marble. In all he showed restraint. Perhaps for a medieval interior of this size even his removal of the low box pews was no bad thing.

Almost all the churchyard tombstones are of slate, some very well lettered; the best, to Ann Jones, born in Boston, New England, in the mid-18th century, lies almost completely hidden by grass beneath the yew trees east of the path leading towards the south transept. Dafydd ap Gwilym, in whose poetry George Borrow found the qualities of Ovid, Horace and Martial combined, was born in the parish about 1320. He diverted the stream of Welsh poetry from the narrow Bardic tradition of north Wales with its emphasis on the exploits of princes, the praise of victory, and the lamentation of defeat into the broader waters of everyday life. South Walian by birth and with a Norman background, he sang of nature and love with a frank, sensual hedonism which has since furrowed many a Calvinist brow. He admitted going to church to pick out the pretty faces in the congregation; for him pleasure came from Heaven and sorrow from Hell. To scholars of European medieval poetry he ranks very high. For a fascinating essay on his work see *The Development of Welsh Poetry* by Sir H. Idris Bell (Clarendon Press, Oxford).

Llanbadarn Odwyn (6). The church of St Padarn lies remotely off the Roman road *Sarn Helen* which bisects this parish of small farms and wide vistas. It is a primitive building on a foundation of large boulders with few windows and no porch. The interior, a single chamber, is bare except for altar, pews, reading desk, harmonium and chancel chairs. After disuse it was reopened in 1952. Typical of so many upland Welsh parishes, there is little sign of human habitation and nothing approaching a village nucleus.

Llanbadarn Trefeglwys (5). *Pennant* in the north of the parish is a charming valley hamlet of cottages, the cool *Ship Inn*, an ancient stone bridge over the Arth and, matching all, a cream and beige Methodist chapel (1768–1883) in the early 19th-century manner, with tall round headed windows; the interior has tiered pews, a gallery and in the vestibule partition a window of about sixty small panes of coloured glass, blues, reds, greens with some clear, which would look well in a West End art gallery. A mile away on the Aberaeron road, the parish church of St Padarn was enlarged and largely rebuilt in 1905. It is a plain, rough-cast, single chamber of no special interest except for the reredos, which was given in the 1920s by fourteen men from the district who were all in the ministry of the Church at that time; they included Timothy Rees, Principal of the College of the Resurrection, Mirfield, before he became Bishop of Llandaff.

Monachty, south of Pennant, is the principal house of the parish. Its elegant Georgian south elevation of two storeys, long sash windows and central pediment can be admired over the parkland from the deep stone bridge sprouting with ferns, in the valley below. John Nash the architect was a friend of the Gwynne family which once owned this estate.

Llanbadarn y Creuddyn Lower (5). A small parish without a village nucleus, and trisected by two good roads which converge at South Gate on the outskirts of Aberystwyth. Its northern boundary is the Rheidol valley along whose southern ridge runs the fast A.4120 road to Devil's Bridge. On it are parking places with rewarding views of valley, coast and town and the distant northern mountains. Over the ridge to the south, Paith valley is richly wooded along a good branch road to Trawscoed and the Ystwyth valley. The feature of the parish is *Nanteos* mansion, set on the floor of the Paith valley in the shelter of a steep and finely timbered slope. It can be seen to advantage through hedgegaps on the Trawscoed road across its wide parkland. Open to visitors during summer on Wednesday and Bank Holiday afternoons, it is approached down a shady side road and past a pretty Victorian lodge in Papworth's Cheltenham Italianate style. Nanteos (in English, nightingale's stream but no nightingale has been heard there in living memory) is one of the notable Georgian houses of Wales, but because of its dark masonry not among the more beautiful. Built in 1739 its main block is a solid stone faced rectangle of three storeys about one hundred feet long and seventy-five feet wide with a balustraded parapet carrying urns. Unfortunately much of the detail of the front elevation, including some of the decorated window heads and the bulls' eye windows of the attic storeys, is hidden under Virginia creeper, and the comparison with a hydro is inescapable. The interior has been little

The stables at Nanteos,
LLANBADARN Y CREUDDYN
LOWER

LLANDDEWI BREFI

altered since the 18th century, and the first floor salon is particularly distinguished for its excellent plaster work and original gold leaf decoration, revealed by recent renovation. Richard Wagner visited Nanteos and is said to have composed part of his opera *Parsifal* there. Lord Byron and Swinburne were other visitors. Among the relics shown to visitors are the remains of a dark olive wood cup with healing properties, linked by tradition either to the cup used at the Last Supper, brought by Joseph of Arimathea to Glastonbury and thence by the monks of Strata Florida, or to the cup of vinegar given to Christ on the Cross. There

are fine hatchments on the stairway walls. It is certainly worth coming a long way to see the stable block and its entrance screen. The latter appears to belong to the Greek Revival period at the beginning of the 19th century, reproducing detail from the main block and is attributed locally to either C. R. or S. P. Cockerell. The entrance arch is high, flanked by Doric columns and entablature, and the screen is topped by stone figures of a horse in the centre and eagles with outstretched wings on either side. The stable and coach-house doors are round arched under wide eaves. A cupola rises from the roof opposite the entrance. The yard

remains cobbled. There are poignant smells for horse lovers and no evidence of "improvement".

Llanbadarn y Creuddyn Upper (3). A narrow parish starting at *Capel Seion* on the A.4120 Aberystwyth to Devil's Bridge road and taking in the southern slopes of the Rheidol valley with all its splendid precipitous scenery. A small valley settlement at *Abernant* on the narrow gauge Vale of Rheidol railway with a nearby 1844 Methodist chapel. The *Central Electricity Power Station* is upstream from Abernant. Two great water-driven turbines help to generate electricity for the grid system. The landscaping of the reservoir and the Central Electricity property at *Felin Newydd* has earned a Civic Trust award.

Llancynfelin (2). Where the floods of pre-history receded, small mounds and ridges were left above the flat expanse of marshy land; on one of these the hamlet which gives the parish its name is sited. It consists of a farm or two and the church of St Cynfelin (the name is related to the British King Cunobelinus, Shakespeare's Cymbeline). A small bellcote rubble building with a south transept, its 13th-century fabric can be dated from a blocked doorway in the south wall. It was completely restored by the Victorians. A picture of the earlier seating, with pulpit and reading desks against the centre of the north wall, hangs in the vestry. Medieval bits are the 14th-century font bowl, and a piece of the rood screen now serving as a canopy of the reredos, both recovered from a nearby farm. Lancet of the Virgin by Martin Travers (1938) and a brass tablet (1810) to Jane Gilbertson of a kneeling woman, and in Gothic lettering the prayer from her lips "that they also shall rest in hope". A pretty, weathered little church in a circular churchyard.

Away from the flat land the parish extends to the western slopes of the Plinlimon range. Beyond the main road, at *Tre'r ddol*, the 1845 *Soar* Wesleyan chapel in classical Georgian style has been turned into a local museum. The religious revival of 1859, led by the Rev. Humphrey R. Jones, started in this chapel, which now houses a collection of religious documents and books on Methodism, objects of local interest and a collection of modern pictures.

Borth Bog, Cors Fochno, occupies much of the parish, a flat expanse of scrub, grazing and plough land. Some two hundred acres of it, a sort of no man's land to which no title can be established, have been scheduled as a national nature reserve. The whole is of great scientific interest, a rare example of a raised bog of wet, acid peat. It holds many varieties of mosses, including the rare Sphagnum Imbricatum, a peat forming moss. Seventy-four kinds of moths and butterflies and twenty-two kinds of breeding birds have been identified. Polecats are quite common.

Llanddeinol (5). A small parish of some two thousand acres opening inland from the cliffs of Cardigan Bay. The church of St Deinol, rebuilt early in the 19th century and restored in 1883 has a squat west end tower and an apsidal east end. Its furniture is late Victorian but the east end is quite showy and has Kempe style glass in three of the lancet windows. Below, the village school and attached house make a fine solid group.

Llanddewi Aberarth (5). A huddle of houses in the narrow lanes of an old fishing village, separated by meadow land from the shore of Cardigan Bay. The Arth cuts a deep ravine which is spanned by the main coast road, where Methodist chapel *Bethel* (1805–48) is showy with red paint and formal in its square sashed windows and double doors. On the hills behind, the tower of the 13th-century church of St David presides over the landscape. Its modernised interior is neat and clean, the walls blue and grey washed, and the pews golden grained. An early 19th-century tablet to the memory of David Jones, vicar for fifty-four years, has a verse with the opening line "*Within these sacred walls I spent my breath.*" There are pieces of an ancient stone shaft in the porch.

Tyglyn, in the southern corner of the parish above the right bank of the river Aeron, is an unspoilt 17th-century house, stone built, of two storeys with sash and dormer windows. Its records go back to the 11th century. A single chamber private chapel forming the north wing was unfortunately stripped of its furniture by a previous occupant, but the gallery remains. There are splendid trees in the park and a fine herd of Welsh Black cattle. At the end of the 18th century Miss Jones, heiress of Tyglyn, married the Rev. Alban Thomas, heir of Lewis Gwynne of Monachty in the neighbouring parish of Llanbadarn Trefeglwys. When the latter died, his store of gold, to the then value of £100,000, was taken by horse sledge from Monachty to Tyglyn. Mr and Mrs Thomas, who had taken the name of Gwynne, used much of their newly acquired fortune in the development of Aberaeron as a port for the hinterland of the Aeron valley.

Llanddewi Brefi (9). Beautiful setting at an opening of the mountains west of Tregaron and the Abergwesin pass. The mountain road runs from here, after joining Sarn Helen, to *Farmers* in Carmarthenshire. Tracts of the uplands have been recently planted by the Forestry Commission. The village is important in the history of the Celtic Church because St David was called here to refute the heresy of Pelagius, who denied the doctrine of original sin. As St David started to speak, the ground rose beneath him to form a platform, where the church now stands, and a white dove settled on his shoulder.

The 13th-century church of St David, once cruciform, has herringbone masonry and central tower but the transepts have gone. The grandeur of proportions remains, in spite of restoration amounting almost to rebuilding. Early 19th-century pews have been pickled, and have lost their doors. One or two "churchwarden" Gothick windows left, but the whole is very much swept and garnished. The long and imposing interior is dominated by a strident (recent) east window, and against the west wall there is a 1959 statue of St David by A. Mancini.

The village—almost a small town —is attractive and well disposed, somewhat dwarfed by the tall church, with bridge, whitewashed cottages and gay gardens. Chapel with double doors and elegant marbling. The swelling slopes to the east have fine trees in the hedgerows. Hillside quarry.

The Roman site of *Bremia* or *Loventium* in the fields of Llanio Issa farm awaits further excavation; nothing of it remains above ground. A building stone with marks of the Second Cohort of the Asturians, an auxiliary regiment of the Roman army, was found in a barn of Llanio Issa farm and is now in the National Museum, Cardiff. How, one wonders, did Asturians fare in this distant land, within sight of the mountain ranges, so similar in outline to those at home?

Llandre (2). The main centre of *Geneu yr Glyn* parish, a prosperous-looking village on the railway to Aberystwyth, bright with new bungalows. St Michaels parish church, bellcote and rebuilt in 1884, looks over it from a tree-covered hillside. It is approached through an 18th-century stone lychgate, round-arched at each end, and slate tombstones climb the steep churchyard to hanging woods. There are two windows by Roy Lewis, 1962 and 1963, stark and a bit original; one in blue, black and white glass only. The east window is by Whitefriars—not bad—and there are 18th-century wall tablets. Furnishing is entirely late Victorian.

The lane to the south-east of the churchyard leads to hill-top *Castell Gwalter*, a motte mound and stronghold of the Norman Walter de Bec, six hundred feet above sea level with commanding views. The way to it through a field can be very damp.

There is a valley settlement with a hump back, single-arched bridge over the river Leri at *Dolybont* and, up the valley, *Felin Fawr* millhouse, L shaped and late 18th-century. Caravans nearby. On the high ground to the north from the road to Talybont are splendid views of the Snowdon range and the broken line of hills in the foreground.

Llandyfriog (7). A.475 to Lampeter leaving the course of the Teifi rises steeply into sparse and featureless country; similarly a secondary road climbs towards the coast from the outskirts of Newcastle Emlyn. The village is a long straggle of hillside cottages, often bright as a child's painting, parallel to and overlooking the valley. The principal house is *Cilgwyn*, in fine parkland, built in the 1870s (architect, Stuart of Bath). It was designed in Gothic style to accommodate a prize-winning wooden staircase from the Paris exhibition of 1867. The ballroom floor is laid on five railway buffers and has a rise and fall of nine inches. The house is now used mainly for Nonconformist conferences.

The church of St Dyfriog on the right bank of the Teifi was built in 1890 (architect, Middleton of Cheltenham) on a simple nave and chancel plan, with plenty of light through clear glass windows and better-than-average 1930 stained glass in the east window. Hatchment and tablets (four of them removed from St Mary's Church, Paddington) of the Fitzwilliams and related families of Cilgwyn. Opposite the west wall the tombstone of Thomas Heslop (1780–1814), victim of the last duel fought in Wales, has a suitably peremptory epitaph "*Alas poor Heslop*" and no other inscription.

Llandygwydd (7). The church of St Tugwydd, grouped on a wooded bank with the slate-built village school, was completely rebuilt in 1856 (architect, R. J. Withers) in lofty Gothic. Its tower originally carried a spire, which collapsed shortly after completion. Inside is an elaborate Decorated reredos with matching pulpit and font, and heavily stained glass from the 1850s onwards in every window. High on a vestry wall is an 18th-century tablet to the Parry family of Noyadd Trefawr, with cherubs and painted arms, and others include two in classical style by D. Mainwaring, Carmarthen. At *Ponthirwaun* are a disused mill and an 1840 *Bethesda* Congregational chapel, with hipped roof, white plastered front and new ceiling, but original furniture, and monkey puzzle tree. At this charming (despite inevitable corrugated iron) hamlet, above the bridge a pathway leads to a glimpse of the Picturesque in miniature—a stream falling over boulders between slatey walls in which heather and scrub oak are firmly bedded. For the Picturesque on a grander scale, see the famous falls and pools of the Teifi at *Cenarth* on the county boundary.

Penylan is the best of the many country houses in the Teifi valley; added to an earlier house in the 1830s on the proceeds of compensation paid when the Skerries Lighthouse off Anglesey was taken over by Trinity House, it adorns its splendid position. Inside, a fine suite of lofty rooms on the ground floor has ceilings painted and decorated by Italian craftsmen; one has garlands of flowers native in the district. From a large hall floored in light coloured stone in diamond pattern, a cantilever staircase of similar stone rises to the second floor, where a small balcony with marble pillars opens a view of the hall below. *Noyadd Trefawr* is another good house with a 19th-century front of sashed windows, six gabled dormers and a Gothic porch. An earlier interior has two panelled rooms. Behind, a still earlier and primitive farmhouse with large open fireplace. *Blaenpant*, mainly 18th century and now partly in ruins, has a panelled room with carved wood swags and an imposing pediment front with long sash windows. On the main road through the Teifi valley, *Llwynduris*, now a hotel, is a low late Georgian house of two storeys, part of which is been demolished. Cork tree in grounds.

Llandyssul (8). More than a village but hardly a town, rising dramatically in oblique terraces from a dark gorge where, below an ancient bridge, the Tyweli river meets the Teifi. It has an important agricultural market and was once the centre of a large woollen industry. The main street, steep, narrow and in summer traffic-ridden, is quite ordinary and has two typical 1830 chapel buildings; the *Tabernacle* is grey and white, and the other is now the offices of the Ministry of Labour. There are early 19th-century terraces. The church of St Tyssul is on the right bank of a wide shallow stretch of the Teifi. Its high, medieval west tower makes the rest of the building seem squat but, inside, the lofty pointed tower and chancel arches and the arcades of the two aisles remove this illusion. The whole interior has been left unplastered after rebuilding, and the small undressed stones are so heavily repointed that the effect is overpowering. Early 19th-century tablets, the best by D. Mainwaring, Carmarthen, to the Lloyd family of Alltyrodin. The old New Year's Day (according to the Julian Calendar) is celebrated on January 13th by church services, attended by choirs and congregations from twelve adjoining parishes. They began about a hundred and fifty years ago to replace the annual ball game, in which the same twelve parishes took part, too rowdily for the then vicar's tastes. The change was not welcomed, but the ancient game of quoits is still very popular in the villages around, from Pontshaen to Abergorlech. North of the churchyard a private suspension bridge of slats and sheep netting gives precarious passage into Carmarthenshire.

From Llandyssul two roads run north from the valley into the hinterland of this large parish; A.486, fast but scenically dull though with panoramic views to the east, and B.4589 through Capel Dewi up the beautiful *Cletwr valley*. *Capel Dewi* church (1886, architects Middleton and Prothero, Cheltenham) has a good south front and Victorian stained glass. From the churchyard *Alltyrodin*, the best house in the parish, can be seen to advantage in its lovely setting. It is a large, *c.* 1800, rectangle of three storeys and a portico with Doric columns. The interior has good contemporary features, fine wide staircase, good mouldings and cornices and Adam style fireplaces; classical stables and outbuildings dated 1840. *Rock Mill*, an attractive 1890 stone built group, is one of the few remaining woollen mills in the area to be worked by water power, and on a family basis. Northwards on the B.4589 and A.475 crossroads at *Rhydowen* a square, period-piece, 1834 Unitarian chapel, now closed and friendless, has round-headed double doors and sash windows and interesting slate tombstones built into the front elevation. North again, *Pontshaen* has terraced houses of stone and yellow brick in a dark narrow cleft, like a mining village. This district has been called *Y Smottyn Du* ("The Black Spot") because of Unitarian schisms. A mile north of Pontshaen alongside and directly above B.4489, marked "Castell" on the O.S. map, lies the motte stronghold of Humphrey, one of the early Norman warlords. Poisonous Leopard's Bane, a continental variety not native in Britain, is said to grow on it, possibly a Norman survival. The name of the motte was changed later by conquest to *Castell Hywel* and, in the nearby house of that name, David Davies who translated Gray's Elegy into Welsh was born. Around *Prengwyn* the lanes are hedged with beech trees, and the sloping woods are deep in bluebells.

LLANFIHANGEL Y CREUDDYN
LOWER

The Devil's Bridge Valley, LLANFIHANGEL Y CREUDDYN UPPER

Llanerch Aeron *see* **Ciliau Aeron.**

Llanfair Clydogau (9). A thinly populated, wholly agricultural parish divided by the Teifi, rising to moorland on the south flank of the valley through the recently planted *Llambed* forest, and on to the Roman Road in Cellan parish. North-east of the Roman Road there is fine walking country from above Moelfryn, over Bryn Mawr and on to Garn Fawr which overlooks *Llyn Gwaith*. The views from this ridge are spectacular on either side. Less than half a mile south-west of Bryn Mawr the landscape is broken by a natural rampart

of enormous rocks, so fissured by time and weather as to seem artificially placed. Nearby, to the southeast, is a series of cairns of which only the outlines are visible. In one, however, the burial chamber is plain to see, with the side stones still vertically in position and the capstone lying to one side. It is worth searching out as an example of a Bronze Age burial chamber.

Out of the valley the lanes are few and narrow. The church of St Mary, in a circular churchyard by the side of the main valley road, was rebuilt in 1888 with an imposing double bellcote. Its Perpendicular windows

are better than average for this type of church and the glass at the east end is by Celtic Studios; otherwise plenty of light through clear glass windows makes this a very pleasant church, although the simple pews are rather heavily varnished. An ancient font bowl, possibly pre-Norman, rests on a brick base. It has four projecting, roughly carved stone images; one of a human face, another, the best, of a bird like a curlew and the other two, indistinct,

Falls of the Mynach, Devil's Bridge

probably of beasts. Across the river which is spanned by a low stone bridge, Congregational *Capel Mair* next to the village shop is a simple 1823–45 stone-faced building with double doors and square upper windows. The interior is plain, with the usual low box pews of the period, heavily grained; but how admirably the whole fits its site.

Llanfihangel y Creuddyn Lower (6). The village of grouped, late 18th-century cottages, and a four square house with massive chimney stacks shows little alteration for two hundred years. It is levelly sited in green, gentle country of small farms and narrow lanes, dominated by the heavy central tower and short spire of the 13th-century cruciform church (St Michael), a welcome change from bellcote churches. The interior is heavily plastered, and all the lancet windows are of clear or tinted glass. The most striking feature, marred by hanging chromium heaters, is the wagon roof, 15th- or 16th-century, covering the whole interior and boarded between the ribs over the chancel. The 1919 reredos is a high relief carving in oak of the Last Supper, by Jules Bernaerts of the Belgian Hamand School of Woodcarving. There are fine yew trees in the churchyard, a wooden sundial on the south wall, and a small 18th-century brass tablet on a low tombstone on the left of the pathway from the porch to the churchyard gate. Beyond the stream south of the church is a pretty little village school (1838 and 1875), with louvred spire. From the hill between the village and *Cnwch Goch* is Swiss valley scenery of bare, green, crinkled slopes and forestry plantations, with Trawscoed mansion to the right in Llanafan parish. South along the road to Pontrhydygroes are surrealist backgrounds of smooth, grey lead-mine spoil, with ruined fortress-like buildings against bare hills.

Llanfihangel y Creuddyn Upper (6). Endowed by Nature with all the elements of the Picturesque. At *Devil's Bridge* the level of the main road has been twice raised, so that three bridges, the lowest one medieval, are visible, and the river Mynach falls in a series of vertical cascades.

In flood it becomes a gigantic waterfall of five hundred feet into the valley where it is joined by the Rheidol, flowing from Plinlimon in the other direction. Carefully made steps and bridges allow good views from many points. Above the scrub-covered gorge are taller trees, and above them glimpses of green hills, some gently rounded and others shaped like cones and nipples. The chasm is clearly confined and contained—a different world from that beyond its bounds.

> "I seem to stand
> as in life's morn; permitted to behold,
> from the dread chasm, woods climbing above woods
> in pomp that fades not."

Permission to behold would today cost Wordsworth a shilling. Turnstiles modify the shock of surprise.

Above the ravine stands the *Hafod Arms Hotel*, rebuilt by the fourth Duke of Newcastle in the 1830s; a Swiss chalet of grey stone with amazingly wide, bracketed eaves. Many come here in the summer by the narrow gauge Vale of Rheidol railway from Aberystwyth, twelve miles away. At *Capel Bangor* the line enters the gorge and makes a seven mile ascent of six hundred feet.

The human interest of this remarkable parish lies elsewhere, at *Hafod* in the Ystwyth valley over the moorland south of Devil's Bridge, and in its owner Thomas Johnes (1748–1816). He was the son of a prominent Welsh landowner who had married into a wealthy family, the Knights of Croft Castle near Ludlow. There Thomas Johnes spent most of his youth, and with his cousin Richard Payne Knight and the latter's friend Uvedale Price, he was one of a group of enlightened country gentlemen who followed Price's theories of the Picturesque, one principle of which was that romantic, natural settings demanded a romantic style of architecture on the lines of the great 18th-century landscape paintings. At his father's death, Johnes inherited the Hafod estate and a vast fortune in other property. Turning his back on Croft Castle, he devoted the rest of his active life to Hafod. In this green and primitive valley, almost entirely

surrounded by hills as savage and bare as their impoverished occupants, Johnes saw the making of Arcadia. Restless and indomitable, he poured his money into improving the look of the country and the lot of its people. Guided always by the principles of the Picturesque, he employed the Bath architect Thomas Baldwin to build a new house in the Gothic style, James Wyatt to design a new church, and Fuseli to decorate it. He lured Scottish farmers to bring south their modern agricultural techniques. Bogs were drained, new breeds of cattle imported from England and abroad, and, in a space of six years, over two million trees were planted to give shelter and to improve the landscape. But he must have defied the old gods and in 1807, in the manner of a Greek tragedy, the first calamity struck Hafod. The house, into which Johnes had poured his treasure and which he had filled with works of art, was gutted by fire, and his priceless collection of books in the octagonal library designed by John Nash, where he had translated *Froissart's 'Chronicles'* into English, was lost. Although hard pressed for money, he set about rebuilding it and refurnishing it with treasures bought at the sale of Beckford's Fonthill. In 1811, the second blow, from which no recovery was possible, struck. His beloved daughter Mariamne, crippled from childhood by a spinal disease, died, and with her death went his love of Hafod. Five years later Johnes died at Dawlish in Devon. Hafod and its contents were sold to the Duke of Newcastle; after him it went through various hands, degenerating at each passage, until, in ruins, its parks and hillsides stripped of their timber, it was demolished by gunpowder in 1950. In 1932 a fire starting from an overheated flue destroyed the interior of Wyatt's Gothic church of St Michael, shattering to fragments Chantrey's monument of Mariamne and her parents, which had been commissioned by Johnes and paid for by the Duke of Newcastle, after lying unpaid for in Chantrey's studio.

Now only a heap of rubble marks the site of Hafod in the centre of a

LLANGEITHO

52

small caravan park. The tragic story of Johnes' life explains the melancholy which hangs over this silent and deserted place.

Wyatt's church was reroofed and refurnished under the direction of W. D. Caröe, who seems consciously to have tried to relieve the sadness of the fragments of Chantrey's monument, now piled in the north transept. Pieces of medieval Flemish glass, saved from the fire, have been replaced in the east window.

Up the Ystwyth valley as far as *Blaencwm*, where the bridge, built by Thomas Baldwin, still spans the river, there is desolation of abandoned lead and silver mine workings; the hillsides are marked with the spoil from tunnelled mines, like rabbit scrapes, and the ground so thick with stones that Nature cannot cover its nakedness.

South-west of Devil's Bridge and over the fields from *Fron Goch pool*, which supplied water power to the neighbouring lead mines, the church of St Michael at *Llantrisant* stands isolated and lost on a hilltop with wide views eastward over bare brown hills. All that can be identified of the 13th-century fabric, now heavily plastered on the outside, is the outline of pointed windows. The interior, glimpsed through clear glass, was completely refurnished in the last century. A silent and rather eerie place. To the north is an 1850 Wesleyan chapel and house, and to the south, around *Lletysynod*, the landscape is again scarred and distorted by abandoned mine workings.

Llanfihangel Ystrad (8). In the middle reaches of the river Aeron the hills fall back, leaving between them a valley broken by thin streams among rich meadowland. It is a quiet valley of great beauty against the background of the rounded hills behind *Felindre*, comparable with the Denbighshire Vale of Clwyd. Southward, the main road hugs the flank of the western hills, past a stone, octagonal lodge at the entrance to the long, straight, rhododendroned drive leading to Brynog across the river in Trefilan parish, then past the tall chimney and low buildings of the *Milk Marketing Board* which give the valley a Swiss look, and so to the village centre. Here, in a pretty roadside group of pub with stabling and cottages, the church of St Michael is a simple, bellcoted, late Victorian rebuilding in the style of R. J. Withers. It has many 19th-century memorials on the scraped walls, mostly to soldiers of the Vaughan family, including an imposing Sebastopol tablet by S. Manning, London. Out of the valley the parish, one person to eleven acres, is sparse upland. From *Temple Bar*, south, the main road crosses high ground into the Teifi watershed. Eyecatcher chapel, 1848 Congregational *Rhydigwyn* near Temple Bar, is stark white with black quoins, round headed windows and twin doors below black arches and small sash windows in the upper storey to light a small gallery. The principal house *Llanllyr*, almost on the left bank of the Aeron, is a gabled three storeyed Tudor building with a Regency two storey wing and verandah, in parkland. It is on the site of a Cistercian nunnery.

Llangeitho (5). A shrine of Welsh Calvinistic Methodism; for here Daniel Rowlands (1713–1790), son of the rector of the parish and curate of several parishes including Llangeitho, led from within the Church the great religious revival to bring the Welsh Church into a closer, more native association with the life of the common people. His colleagues were ordained clergy, such as Griffith Jones, vicar of Llandowror in Carmarthenshire, and laymen such as Howel Harris of Talgarth in Breconshire. Their inspiration and eloquence spread a new faith like fire through Wales, fanned by the efforts of the Anglicised Church to quell them. In 1763 Rowlands was suspended from his clerical duties, but he continued to preach in a new building, essentially a preaching house, in Llangeitho—then the "New Church" and now the Calvinistic Methodist chapel —built to take the crowds which came to hear him. He is buried in the parish church of St Ceitho and commemorated by a slate slab to himself, his wife and sister Jennet. His son John became rector of Llangeitho, and his grandson, Daniel, a successful barrister and F.S.A., and builder of *Saxonbury Lodge*, near Frant in Sussex. Another memorial to the revivalist is his marble statue in the foreground of the chapel, a large square building in traditional style.

The village, on the southern boundary of the parish in the Aeron valley, is a nucleus of trim terrace houses, an inn, and conventional First World War Memorial facing a roundabout on the central crossroads. The church, rather aloof from the village, was restored and enlarged in 1900. Shaded by large yew trees, it has early 20th-century stained glass in the east window, other glass by Celtic Studios and Whitefriars, the latter depicting the church in the lower panel, and in a window on the north wall a careful portrait of a bareheaded officer killed in the Great War, dressed as a Roman soldier. But interest centres on the memorial to Daniel Rowlands and the 18th-century tablet—Carreg Rowland— with a Latin inscription to the memory of his parents Daniel and Jennet. North of the church, a lane climbs some six hundred feet to the main Tregaron to Aberaeron road, and the parish peters out into desolate swampland near Llyn Fanod (see *Blaenpennal*).

Llangoedmor (7). B.4570 road eastward from Cardigan bisects the parish. The northern half is open and dull, with no buildings of interest except a striking Baptist chapel (1769–1809–1838) overlooking the coast road at *Penparc*. It has grey and white walls under a hipped slate roof, a black slate name plaque and tiled baptistry. An outlying church at *Tremain* was built in 1848 (architect J. Jones, fitted by R. J. Withers). It is of no interest. High ground above B.4570 gives splendid views southward across the Teifi valley, especially from north of *Pantgwyn*, a good, medium-sized early 19th-century country house of plastered stone under hipped slate roof, with neat sash windows and central chimney stack. South of B.4570 the landscape is broken and wooded and the village consists of the church, a few cottages and two country houses, *Plâs Llangoedmor* built in 1760, with a central pediment, surrounded by splendid trees, and early 19th-century *Treforgan*, also hidden by trees on rising ground, and locally said, with no supporting evidence, to have been designed by John Nash.

The church of St Cyrumo, originally a chapel of the Plâs, was enlarged in the 18th century by the present chancel, the same length as the nave. At their junction a small slate steeple was erected in the style of a Wren city church. Restored in 1860 by R. J. Withers, the interior has conventional late 19th-century furniture, 1950 stained glass—not bad—in east window, and 1930 stained glass by William Glasby on the south wall. Hatchment of Lloyd family of Coedmor and tablets from the 18th century, mainly to Coedmor families, by Barlow of London, F. Read of Pimlico and Wood of Bristol. A mile east of the church, *Cilbronnau*, in parkland, was completely rebuilt in 1910 on the foundations of a much larger building.

The most populated and the best part of the parish is at *Llechryd* where the road from Cardigan comes sharply to the edge of the Teifi, and a massive stone bridge with four cutwaters on each side carries a side road over the river into Pembrokeshire. Llechryd, in the shadow of a hill on which stands *Glanarberth*, a Regency-style mid 19th-century house, has pleasant if minor architectural features such as the closely glazed windows of the *Carpenter's Arms*, and cottages up side roads; also a disused roadside church with low box pews, liable to flooding. There is a pretty sheltered hollow and mill stream and cottages to match below *Glanolmarch* (gabled Tudor Gothic).

Coedmor, off the beaten track, is a mellow, two-storeyed, early 19th-century country house with earlier outbuildings. It is on the site of a hunting lodge of the Lloyd family, on the edge of the ancient forest which gave the house its name. A three-storeyed tower with cupola was added about 1850. The setting, sheer above the Teifi gorge, is as romantic as that of Cilgerran Castle on the opposite bank and from that viewpoint the cupola, peeping out above the trees, adds a special charm.

Llangorwen (or Clarach) (2). On the brow of the hill north of Aberystwyth a side road leads back to the coast (hairpin bend) over an 18th-century stone bridge, past the church and a small group of houses on the open plain; so open that there is no disguising the welter of caravans, chalets and the rest which crowd in on Clarach bay, morose and shingly at high tide, but with good bathing when the tide is out. The 1841 church of All Saints, simple nave and chancel with tall west tower and spire, is notable as being the first church designed by William Butterfield. The well-kept interior is quite beautiful in its simplicity of lancet windows, clear glazing, white plastered walls, the restrained elegance and carving of oak pews, pulpit, reading desk and low chancel screen, contrasting with the ornate design of four bronze chandeliers given by John Keble. The lectern is thought to have been given by John Henry Newman. This link with the Tractarian or Oxford High Church movement comes from the association between the Rev. Isaac Williams (1802–1865), born locally at Cwmcynfelin, and other leaders of the movement. Isaac Williams, poet and theologian, Dean of Trinity College, Oxford, was a curate of Newman at St Mary's Oxford, and a close friend of Keble. He contributed to the series *Tracts for the Times;* his tract no. 80, *Reserve in Communicating Religious Knowledge*, was widely misunderstood, and its reception caused him great bitterness. Disappointed in his hope to succeed Keble as Oxford's Professor of Poetry, he retired from public life to Stinchcombe, Glos., where he died.

Cymcynfelin, now converted into flats, is a tall, late 18th-century house of unplastered stone adorning its beautiful site on the escarpment above the church. North of church a disused mid-Victorian school is worth a glance for the detail of the roof slating and outside cornice.

Llangranog (7). In the south of the parish the main coast road loses its bare character as it moves inland, and trees and woods become welcome. The village on the coast is subdued, also drab in tone, difficult of access and with striking Nonconformist architecture. But the fine stretches of yellow sand, the rock outcrops at low tide, and the accommodation make it a popular resort.

Between July and September more than two thousand children from all over Wales spend a week or more at the annual camp of *Urdd Gobaith Cymru*, the Welsh League of Youth. The principal house, *Pigeonsford*, is a typical late 18th-century Cardiganshire house, with later additions. It can be seen across a valley at the entrance to the village. Imposing 1878 Gothic chapel with elaborate pointed window at *Pentregat* on A.487.

Llangwryfon (5). Desolate and broken moorland around *Trefenter*, and a plain Victorian church (1879 by A. Ritchie, Chester) to the north. The adjoining 1861 National School, now the church hall, is a better building, distinguished by its wide closely latticed windows with clear diamond panes. Down the hill the Methodist chapel has well-spaced sash windows in its vestry and attached buildings.

Llangybi (8). The village street on the main road from Lampeter to Tregaron is mainly terraced with low houses. At its northern end the ancient, bellcote church of St Cybi, in a circular churchyard, was lightly restored about 1895; its outside walls are beautifully weathered, and inside the pointed windows have clear glass with pretty coloured panes in the apex of each; boarded ceiling and low box pews. The Birth, Crucifixion and Ascension are illustrated in good blue, red and green glass in the east window. There is another centre of population to the southwest at *Bettws Bledrws* outside the main gates of Derry Ormond House. The church of St Bledrws was rebuilt except for its medieval tower in 1887. It has two features, a pre-Raphaelite style window in the west wall and a font cover made of strips of oak from St Davids Cathedral, the old church of Bettws Bledrws, Llandinam in Anglesey and Llanbadarn Fawr. Tablets include one by Richard Westmacott Jnr. (1835).

Derry Ormond House, designed by C. R. Cockerell in his classical style and built in 1824, has been demolished, but some outbuildings remain. A circular column with slit windows on high ground to the south of Derry Ormond was built in the 19th century as an eyecatcher, and to give employ-

55

Derry Ormond Tower, LLANGYBI

ment to local people by a member of the Inglis Jones family of Derry Ormond. On the northern slopes of the parish, rush-grown meadows give way to forestry plantations, and the lanes are very narrow.

Llangynllo (8). An inland parish, richly endowed by Nature and the Victorians. Nature provides two lovely valleys, and from the parish church of St Cynllo a view of romantic beauty which, in the Picturesque tradition, the architect R. K. Penson adorned in Rhenish style with *Bronwydd,* built about 1855 for Sir Thomas Davies Lloyd, Bart., Lord Marcher of the Barony of Cemaes in Pembrokeshire, descendant of the Norman Marcher Lord, Martin de Tours. Bronwydd is empty and deserted now, not yet a romantic ruin despite its turrets and pinnacles. The ivy and the flittermice are still to come. *Gernos,* too, has lost its glory. Once a notable Georgian house, later heavily Victorianised. Now the snores of fattening pigs are heard from behind its barricaded doors. A quiet ferny lane dips from *Coedybryn* past the entrance to Gernos down to the hamlet of *Maesllyn,* and its large, stone-built woollen mill.

The interior of the 1870 parish church (could be R. K. Penson: ask for the key at the nearby farm) is rich in late Victoriana, mainly to do with Bronwydd.

Llanilar (5). A narrow, straggling parish, extending to featureless country south of the left bank of the widening Ystwyth river. The valley village is in the English style, with the *Falcon Inn* facing the churchyard and the village stores nearby. *Carmel* (1879) chapel is at a respectful distance past a terrace of decent but darkly decorated houses. 14th-century features of the church of St Hilary are the massive local type west tower, the oak wagon roof (partly renewed), a seven-sided font, and parts of the fabric itself. There is a pre-Norman carved stone in the porch. The interior was restored in 1874 by R. K. Penson. The three-light east window is by Celtic Studios. Framed in Decorated crockets are two Victorian brass tablets to the Williams family of nearby *Castle Hill*, a three-storey building of 1777, with modern glazing and a Venetian window in a low wing. Down a lane, and then across two fields, the sad little 1881 church of St Michael and crumbling school building at *Rhostie* are not worth the rigours of the detour.

Llanina (5). A small parish with a large, formal caravan park and amenities on its western shore. The way to the church, through a wooded valley and then by a footpath through the grounds of Llanina House, has an air of spells and enchantment. The primitive church of St Ina, almost lapped at high tide on a point between two bays, was largely re-built in 1850 from a rebuilding of about 1800. A feature is a beam from a medieval screen across the nave, with carving of a serpentine branch with oak twigs. Stones from an earlier church are incorporated in a stone lychgate. *Llanina House,* an irregular stone and slate roofed two-storey building, once of some con-sequence but now seemingly friend-less, has 17th-century panelling and a wide Jacobean oak staircase from the ground floor to the attics.

Llanio *see* **Llanddewi Brefi.**

Llanllwchaearn (8). Rich Bed and Breakfast country with an occasional Children and Dogs Welcome along the beechy road from *Postmawr* (Synod Inn) through Cross Inn, heralds the approach to New Quay. The hillside church of St Llwchaearn on the outskirts of New Quay is ringed with caravans, and was built in 1865 (architect, R. J. Withers). There is a two-light window by John Hayward of the Draught of Fishes. Typical of the simple nave-and-chan-cel, subdued Gothic of the period, it has better than average modern fur-niture, although the wooden base of the altar table is probably an 1860 medieval reproduction. All that is left of a Royal Arms is a board at the west end, inscribed apparently *Dieu et Mon Dro 1621,* followed by initials. There are also the remains of a very early primitive font.

Llanon *see* **Llansantffraid.**

Llanrhystyd Haminog (5). The only building of interest in this large parish, which straggles from upland marsh to the coast, is *Mabws,* a massive stone built unplastered 18th-century house mainly of three storeys, still very much in its original condition and difficult to maintain. It has an early 18th-century staircase and is romantically hidden among trees on the slope of the upper reaches of *Wyre Fach* valley.

Llanrhystyd Mefenydd (5). The small village lies on a bend of the main coast road at the mouth of the river Wyre. It has some attractive 19th-century and earlier houses, including the two-storeyed Red Lion Hotel. The church of St Rhystyd lies in meadowland off the main road. It was rebuilt about the middle of the 19th century, except for the tower which was then buttressed and topped with a broach spire, out of keeping with native styles. It has a south aisle and chapel, and the in-terior is spacious and light. The chancel and sanctuary have been recently restored. There is an early 19th-century school building on the churchyard boundary. Inland the parish falls on either side into the Wyre valley, and is quite ordinary.

Llansantffraid (5). With *Llanon,* quite a considerable village on both sides of the main coast road. The church of St Bride is apart, close to the water's edge. It is a building of con-siderable character, an early 19th-century single chamber, of impres-sive proportions in the preaching house tradition, with a west gallery, the whole added to the 13th-century tower. The interior, approached through brass-studded green baize doors from a large slate floored porch, is unspoilt late 18th-century—tallish box pews, mercifully clear glass throughout in long windows, and two brass chandeliers in the nave hanging from moulded roundels in the ceiling. There is character out-side, too; a cobbled path from the stile to the west door, lovely weather-ing on the seaward west wall of the tower, and a slate-hung south wall carries a course of long, decorated tombstones, mainly 18th century. The Methodist chapel (1762–1865) at the Llanon end of the village also

has character; it is a gabled building with pediment and pretty moulding, round-headed sash windows and double doors, the whole fading to an attractive grey. Behind the post office, *St Non's chapel* is now little more than a heap of brambles and rubble, but parts of the low, boulder built north and west walls are stand-ing to mark this ancient, possibly 12th-century building.

Off the main road, and on both sides of it, are fishermen's cottages in narrow lanes, and wide-eaved, terrace houses with homely names like "Bryn Awelon" and "Angorfa", where testimonials and pictures of old sailing ships hang on parlour walls, and, behind, snug by kitchen fires, retired ministers and master mariners doze, frowned on by china dogs.

Llantyssiliogogo (8). A large area of scattered hamlets, bisected by A.487 from Plwmp to Postmawr. Best scenery is northwards past *Llwyn-dafydd,* pretty hillside hamlet with inn dated 1799, down the valley to the cliffs and shingle beach at *Cwmtudu,* where caves appear in the cliff face at low tide. The narrow valley is very beautiful with forestry plantations on the steep slopes, and twisted scrub oaks shade the road. North from the beach a road of alarming steepness leads towards the tiny parish church of St Tyssul, which has an unspoilt single-storey cottage to keep it company. These are at the terminus of a No Through Road. The church lacks antiquarian interest, but has a grey weathered look and mild Victorianism inside. There is a pretty, pebble-cast, 1867 chapel at *Nanternis* with a cobbled yard, and a forlorn primitive 1833 one, *Pensarn,* two miles up the lane from Ffynnon Dewi. It is entirely original with low box pews, neatly arranged in tiers, and above the wall clock a Welsh inscription, once not unusual in coastal chapels, *Cofiwch y Morwyr* (remember the sailor), to show that a sailor gave the clock.

The southern half of the parish is divided by the fast A.486 road to New Quay; at the boundary, *Capel Cynon,* the road rises to wide sweeps of bare, downland country. The daughter church of St Cynon is down a lane flanked by a short terrace of

Cwmtudu, LLANTYSSILIOGOGO

gay cottages. Its setting is worth noting, and so is the quality of the slate flooring in chancel and sanctuary. Recast in 1863 by R. J. Williams from an early 19th-century building, its interior is quite modern and simple.

Llanwenog (8). A medley of hamlets are dotted over this large parish—*Cwrt Newydd,* sizeable, terraced and deep in a hollow with large-scale quarrying on one side; *Gorsgoch,* upland and rather grim with an 1861 plain grey washed chapel behind a close array of very Welsh tombstones; *Drefach,* quite ordinary; and the village centre with a good-looking four-square inn and the church of St Gwenog, renowned locally for its antiquity, its 20th-century oak carvings (the bench ends are by a

1914 Belgian refugee and are very good) and the 20th-century chancel screen, well executed but at odds with the 18th-century barrel roof. The antiquarian should be interested in the tall 15th-century tower, its medieval carvings, waterspouts, and armorial emblems; in the painted lettering, on the inside north wall, of the Commandments and Creed in Welsh; in the very early miniature figure of the Crucifixion with the two Marys in the reredos of the modern altar; and in the font, whose round basin is decorated with twelve identical carved faces; unlike other primitive carvings in the district a work of some merit. The church has atmosphere and personality, emphasised by the steep drop from the west entrance by six shallow slate steps to the nave, the cream and

white plastered walls and the massive low arches.

From the nearly circular churchyard there are wide views across the Teifi of the Carmarthenshire hills. The principal house in the parish, *Highmead,* now a County Council Residential School, has been Gothicised with pinnacles and turrets. Llanwenog sheep are a distinct breed, medium sized with brown faces.

Llanwnnen (8). A narrow strip running north from the Teifi and sparsely populated away from the valley. The church of St Gwynnin in the centre of the crossroads hamlet was largely rebuilt except for its

Coybal Bay near NEW QUAY

plain 15th-century tower, in 1877, on the 15th-century foundations.

Llanychaearn (5). On the southern outskirts of Aberystwyth. In its northern corner, west of the A.487 road, the simple bellcote church of St Llwchaearn is beautifully poised above a bend of the swirling Rheidol river, and among close set slate tombstones. Rebuilt and enlarged in 1878, its grey-washed interior is well proportioned. An unobtrusive chancel arch permits a full view of the sanctuary. There are some good memorials and tablets from the 17th century onwards, recording deaths of soldiers and public servants of the Richards and Leir families of Brynyreithin and others, from St Helena to Anzio. Furnishing entirely Victorian, with light coloured stone pulpit and reredos, and stained glass on the south wall by Heaton, Butler and Bayne. Slate tablet on west wall has painted figures with trumpets and red sashes. Painting in oils of original church in porch. The south bay-windowed front of late 18th-century *Brynyreithin,* quite a considerable house for these parts, can be seen across the fields half a mile south of the church.

Llanfarian, on the main coast road, is the chief settlement of the parish; here a bridge crosses the Ystwyth river, and upstream there are two interesting houses near Abermad Weir. The *Manor House,* a plain three-storeyed Georgian house, can be seen from the Llanilar road, white against a rising background of forest; the other, *Abermad House,* to the south, is hidden in the trees. It was built to the design of J. P. Seddon in 1871 of local purplish stone; Gothic in style, it reproduces many of the features of Seddon's work in Aberystwyth University College. It is now a boys' prep school.

Llechryd *see* **Llangoedmor.**

Lledrod Issa or Upper (6). There is a good view of Tregaron Bog from between Ystrad Meurig and *Swydd Ffynon,* a dismal, roadside hamlet with a massive and gloomy Methodist chapel of 1837, and crumbling empty cottages. The road on to A.485 traverses a marsh of pasture-land, rushes and clumps of alders.

Lledrod Ucha or Lower (6). The bellcote church of St Michael was almost entirely rebuilt in 1875 and its only ancient feature is a plain square font basin in the porch; but in the east window there is a splendid, richly coloured, late Victorian stained glass window with pre-Raphaelite feeling, curiously dedicated by Lilian Gilchrist Thompson to the memory of her great-great grandparents who died in 1790 and 1791. Otherwise this pocket handkerchief of a parish is without interest.

Melindwr (3). A narrow central parish east of Aberystwyth; in the moorland on its north-eastern boundary, *Nant y Moch,* a newly flooded valley, is the main reservoir of the Rheidol hydro-electric complex; water is led from it in tunnels to generating stations at Dinas near Pont Erwyd and in the Rheidol valley south-east of Capel Bangor on the road to Aberffrwd. There are a few houses alongside the main road at *Capel Bangor,* and quite a sizeable, open-plan church of about 1830 with pleasant modern fittings and open screen; and on the opposite side of the main road a demure, lattice-windowed village school. Eastward, a lane falls steeply off A.44 through *Goginan* village to the wide valley floor, strewn with the debris of abandoned lead workings: a good

LLANWENOG

60

Goginan, MELINDWR

site for the industrial archaeologist. Two chapels, 1864 Methodist, and plainer 1842 Baptist Jezreel. A new mountain road from Pont Erwyd to Talybont (see *Cwmrheidol* and *Llandre*) is carried over the Nant y Moch dam and in the adjacent and spacious parking ground you can get your bearings from a thoughtfully-provided and well-executed relief map in moulded metal. On all sides the scene is one of mountain grandeur.

Mwnt (or Mount) *see* **Verwick.**

Nantcwnlle (5). A large moorland parish with no village except a few cottages, post office and garage at *Bwlchllan,* north of the Aeron valley. The parish church of St Gwynlleu (by A. Ritchie, 1887) lies off the Talsarn road and is saddened by yew trees, heavy early 20th-century stained glass, and general dampness, but there is a good valley view from the west door. The 18th-century pulpit from an earlier church stands forlorn in a corner of the pretty little school building nearby, now the church hall. In the north of the parish is a 1913 corrugated iron

mission church on the B.4576 road near *Penuwch.* Blackgame have been seen on the desolate moorland here, and there are splendid views northward. Daniel Rowlands (see *Llangeitho*) was born in the parish, and was later its curate.

New Quay (5). The New Quay Harbour Company, formed in 1833, established this natural harbour, under the lee of a hill and in a perfect arc of Cardigan Bay, as a trading port and gave impetus to an already growing shipbuilding industry. Within a year or two a pier had been built: John Rennie submitted designs for it which, it seems, were partially followed. In 1857 the main warehouse and sailstore were built on the quayside, a well-proportioned four-storey building with horizontal bands, now converted into an hotel. By 1860 more than six hundred shipwrights were at work, but gradually trade passed to railway and road transport, until eventually the assets of the Harbour Company passed to the Urban District Council, who assumed responsibility for the maintenance of the harbour works, and deserve much credit for the present condition and appearance of them. A lighthouse at the pier end was blown down in 1937, and the pier was extensively repaired and a short jetty added in 1952/3.

Now the summer tourists have taken over, mingling with the retired sea captains and assuming, as of right, the "old salt" look common to British seaside visitors. In peak months the town is at times impenetrable, despite all that the local authority is doing. But out of season you could have nothing better for a quiet holiday; indeed it is one of the pleasantest small resorts on the west coast.

On the trim, brightly painted terraces the architecture is almost entirely 19th-century and except for the ring of caravans and an occasional "shoppe", modern development is unobtrusive and controlled. The terraces rise from the sea level like the tiers of an amphitheatre.

The church is in Llanllwchaearn parish, and the most imposing chapel is *Towyn* Congregational, 1860, of stone blocks with large round-headed windows and a brick and stucco apse.

Orllwyn (8). A parish of rush-grown fields and steep woods. Settlement centres are at *Penrhiwllan,* bleak and unprepossessing; *Aberbanc,* where the main road falls sharply into a valley of pleasant cottages; this has a good Congregational chapel (1794–1864) in Classical style of soft greenish-grey stone blocks, with tall round-headed windows in the gabled front, and original pews and pulpit; and *Henllan* where the road to the valley skirts a mess of wartime huts to a dark silent gorge of the Teifi, spanned by an ancient bridge. There are three churches within a small area, *Llanfair* (St Mary), *Bangor* (St David), and *Henllan* (St David). They are simple bellcote buildings of no special interest except for ancient fonts at the first two. Henllan, rebuilt in 1813, is the earliest.

The principal house, *Blaendyffryn,* has suffered from the addition of a late Victorian three-storey wing to a once charming, wide-eaved, two-storey, late Georgian house.

Penbryn (7). A steep and narrow lane leads from a string of caravan sites to the sandy *Tresaith* beach and a rather untidy huddle of houses and sheds. *Glandwr,* nearby, said locally to have been designed by John Nash, is a small two-storey early 19th-century house with pointed windows on the ground floor. Plastered conical vault to skylight above central landing. A better approach to the sea is through *Sarnau,* from which a lane along the hillside follows the deep valley of wind-blown, stunted sycamore, ash and thorn to end in a wide, sandy beach, backed by sand dunes below slate cliffs covered with gorse and bracken.

The village church of St Michael is on the southern hillside, a medieval building, probably as early as the 13th century, with original, single-light windows in the chancel and north wall of the nave. The interior is quite delightful. The nave, whose width is emphasised by the outward slope of the north wall, has primrose plastered walls, plain grey pews with tomato red ends under a fine medieval collar braced roof of time-bleached oak. The pointed grey washed chancel arch opens to a large and slightly offset chancel under a grey panelled ceiling and with a red ochre east wall. The flooring is almost entirely of large slate slabs. Memorials include a 1645 brass plate on the chancel floor, a 17th-century tombstone and early 19th-century tablets. Near the north wall of the churchyard is the tomb of Anne Adaliza Puddicombe (1836–1908) who, as Allen Raine, wrote Victorian romantic novels of Welsh country life, *By Berwyn Banks,* etc. East of the church is the square Regency house of *Troedyrhiw,* ochre plastered. Below the church, *Pencwm,* a long, low early 19th-century cottage with round-headed windows, is an eyecatcher.

A local fancy,
Penrhiwllan, ORLLWYN

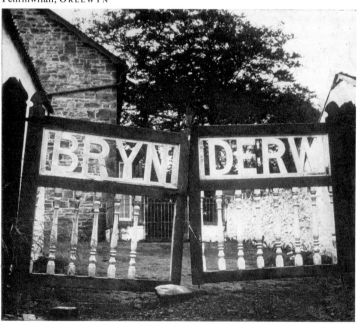

Fainc Ddu, PLINLIMON

On the Sarnau to Tresaith road, in a field of *Dyffryn Bern* farm and marked on the 1-inch O.S. map, stands a Latin inscribed stone, refreshingly on its original tumulus site, and not removed to some church porch.

South of the coastal road, which bisects this large parish, is a picturesque mill group at *Brithdir* on the Ceri stream. The millhouse, whose machinery has been dis-mantled, has a stone with a carved head dated 1786. Another pretty group is at *Glenarthen,* dominated by a large, gabled-fronted mid 19th-century Congregational chapel with primrose plastered front, and usual long round-headed windows and double doors. The nearby village school and school house (1877) is an attractive single unit.

Plinlimon (Punlumon) (3). Black's *Guide to Wales* (1866) says: "Few travellers who make the ascent deem themselves recompensed for the toil and hazard. Not only is the height greatly exceeded by Cader Idris and Snowdon but the scenery exhibited here is inferior both in beauty and grandeur, consisting chiefly of track-less sheep downs of Montgomery-shire, and the barren turbaries of Cardiganshire. All the adjacent hills are destitute of wood, and the whole

PONTRHYDFENDIGAID

scene has a desolate and cheerless aspect."

The reaction to scenery changes. A hundred years has passed since these remarks, and it is reasonable to enjoy the view of the barren turbaries of Cardiganshire spread out from the top of Plinlimon towards Cader Idris—as unsullied and treeless a tract as one can see anywhere in the British Isles, big and bold in effect, and beautifully subject to light and shadow. Trees in the view are, in fact, confined to one small Forestry Commission coppice of firs, some miles to the north-west, so isolated that it looks as if it must have some special reason—it houses the mausoleum of a Welsh chieftain perhaps! The sea is marked by the fringe of caravans north of Aberystwyth. In a few years the scene will be much changed again. The planting to the west is proceeding fast. There are fewer rocks and other signs of wildness than on most Welsh mountains, and the animal and bird life is perhaps sparser, no doubt owing to the treelessness.

An easy approach is now from the road that approaches the big new *Nant y Moch* lake to the west, which is being popularised as a scenic attraction and is newly planted about by the Forestry Commission. *Faincddu*, above the new lake to the east, is the nearest rocky bastion to Plinlimon and, beyond, a steep slope, with some scree, rises to the cairn above it. A new road has been made for the water-supply pipe for Aberystwyth from the lake under the north face of the peak, *Llyn Llygad Rheidol*. This is much like any other lake under a Welsh peak, but the scenery at lake level is fairly tame, and has been further tamed by the recent water-supply attentions—dam, and straightening of banks.

Pont Erwyd *see* **Cwmrheidol.**

Pontrhydfendigaid (6). Originally a riverside settlement on the banks of the Teifi, it is now a typical Welsh village, fairly well contained along the fast Tregaron to Devil's Bridge road. It has strong cultural connections. An annual Eisteddfod, now a two-day affair, attracts large crowds and the distinct Welsh personality is reinforced by a First World War

Memorial (female figure inside black and white iron railings), and an imposing 1859, stone built, Methodist chapel with a gabled front and long, round-headed windows on three sides. The river bridge relieves the scenic monotony, as does an incongruously good Georgian fronted house in the main street. A large village hall built in 1956, the gift of Sir David James (see below), imparts a sense of community. A library and reading room is annexed; it has a 1964 stained glass window by Hardman showing an impressive portrait of Lady James and, in Welsh, an inscription that the window was given by Sir David James in honour of his family.

The parish church of St Mary is a little over a mile to the east of the village, at the entrance to the beautiful *Glasffrwd* valley and in the grounds of *Strata Florida Abbey*. The abbey was founded in the 12th century by the Cistercian Order, whose simple piety and skill in agriculture endeared it to the native Welsh. A leaflet available on the site, now under the guardianship of the Ministry of Public Building and Works, gives the history and layout of the abbey church, little of which remains above ground except for the elaborate, deeply recessed, round-headed west doorway. An 18th-century farm house now occupies much of the monastery site; its weathered and extensive outbuildings enhance the rural beauty of the scene. A ground floor room of the house is panelled, and has over the fireplace a primitive allegorical picture of a Temptation.

St Mary's church was rebuilt about 1815 as a single porchless chamber with a west gallery and pointed windows, within the classical convention of the period. A pulpit dated 1724 remains from the earlier church, as

Tombstone at Strata Florida, PONTRHYDFENDIGAID

65

do the curved communion rails, happily stripped of their black paint in a 1961 redecoration. There is still plenty of light through clear glass on the yellow walls, and it is hoped that a tendency to medievalise this charming classical survival with rich stained glass, however good, will not be carried too far. The Whitefriars windows were given in 1961 by the late Sir David James, who left nearby *Pantyfydwen* farm to join a family business in London, and whose gifts to religion and culture in Wales have been so notable. Early 18th-century tablets include two to Nanteos families who came into the abbey property through marriage with the Stedmans, who acquired it at the Dissolution. Outside, in a well-tenanted churchyard, a large yew tree is said to cover the grave of the great 14th-century poet Dafydd ap Gwilym (see *Llanbadarn Fawr*); he is also commemorated by a large slate monument on the abbey site. Near the yew tree, and incised on a tombstone, is the outline of a leg and thigh and the inscription, "The leg and part of the thigh of Henry Hughes, Cooper, was cut off and interred here June 18th, 1756". Hughes, injured in a stage coach spill, later emigrated to America.

Strata Florida has quiet beauty, but to the east there are darker spells, and the landscape changes dramatically; here an arc of steep, bare hills enfolds a group of five lakes, of which *Llyn Teifi* is the largest. The aspect of the country around the lakes is remarkable; as if some gigantic hand has taken it up, kneaded it, and put it down again. Except that the tops are gently rounded, it reproduces in miniature the features of an Alpine range, contorted and broken by Nature's convulsions, with the suggestion of sudden deep chasms below the five sheets of water, so near to one another and yet so distinct against their bare backgrounds. All around are rocks and stones, tilted, flat or terraced, deeply scored by the strata lines of their original mud and silt deposits.

The route by car to the lakes is from the Cross Inn, *Ffair Rhos,* on the road (B.4343) to Devil's Bridge. It is now metalled to the shore of

Strata Florida Abbey

Llyn Teifi; a little way beyond, it reverts to the old drovers' trail between the abbey and the east, marked on the O.S. map as an ancient road, which, now impassable, crosses the ravine-scored desert over to the Wye Valley. The *Cross Inn* is an eyecatcher, its quoins and keystones decorated in black tracery on a white ground.

The Forestry Commission has now opened a road, unmetalled but passable, south-east from Strata Florida and shown in the O.S. map as a track. It links up with the Abergwesin to Tregaron mountain road.

Pontrhydygroes *see* **Yspytty Ystwyth.**

Silian (8). Tiny parish, reaching north from the Lampeter to Tregaron road into bare mountain land. On the hillside St Sulien's church was almost entirely renewed

Farm at Strata Florida

by R. J. Withers in 1873. It has a neat west spire, nave and chancel; 1930-ish stained glass in the east window in memory of the Stewart family, by A. E. Lemmon, Bromsgrove (John Stewart was schoolmaster here). The stained glass in the north window is by Celtic Studios. Ancient stones, one with a Latin inscription on the south-west corner of the outer wall, and another, decorated, in the vestry.

Strata Florida *see* **Pontrhydfendigaid.**

Talybont *see* **Ceulany Maes Mawr.**

Tirymynach (3). Roadside development and a handsome chapel at *Bow Street* on A.487 at the western boundary of the parish. From Penrhyngoch in Trefeirig parish, a road rises steeply to the north to join a narrow, lonely ridgeway bordered by

sheep cropped downland towards Elerch. There is a small settlement at *Bont Goch;* chapel, charming cottage-post office, and, opposite, a large, well-composed, modern building in imitation stone with concrete lattice screens. It is the filter house for water coming from *Llyn Craig y Pistyll,* on the north-eastern boundary of the parish, and the source of the river Leri. The lake is now a reservoir from which the flow is regulated.

Beware of the narrow track from Bont Goch running south of the bare *Leri* ravine and high above it. It is a rally driver's nightmare, but if you dare take your eyes off the loose track which is deeply scored by hillside floods, the ravine views are even more terrifying and there are no passing places. The track eventually skirts *Pond Syfrydin* in the middle of which rises a circular, verdant tumulus on which gulls breed. Also all around in this bare rushy landscape there are plovers in abundance. A swing to the right at Pond Syfrydin will bring you to the metalled mountain road to Pont Erwyd going south, or the Aberystwyth road going north.

Trefeirig (3). There is no village settlement in this long narrow parish never much more than three miles wide, running across the county from the Plinlimon range on its eastern boundary to the estate of Gogerddan four miles from Cardigan Bay. *Llygad Rheidol* lake, source of the river Wye, can be seen from the southern ascent of Plinlimon Fawr, greenish blue in colour, very deep and beset by huge rocks. *Gogerddan,* for generations the home of the Pryse family (Sir Richard Pryse married the widow of the painter Van Dyck), is a two-storeyed irregular block of late Georgian date, now splendidly maintained and adapted internally as the offices and laboratories of the *Welsh Plant Breeding Station* of the University College of Wales, Aberystwyth. This establishment, which also controls experimental work at neighbouring and outlying lowland and hill farms, will always be associated with the name of Sir George Stapledon, who more than any other man can claim to have made two grasses grow

where one grew before. His portrait by A. Gwynne Jones hangs in the house. On the road from Gogerddan to Penrhyngoch there is a pretty little Gothic cottage with pointed windows and doors and elaborate sash traceries.

Penrhyngoch, a hamlet with some red brick houses, is growing into a village with modern and not unpleasant bungalow development. Its church of St John, 1882, has a high nave with a short, west-end wooden belfry tower, spire and weathercock. Cement rendered walls inside, and an unusual lectern of eagle and serpent in Doulton type pottery on a Coade stone pedestal; glowing three light east window, partly obscured by 1920-ish marble reredos of The Last Supper; two light, early 20th-century stained glass by Hardman in south window of chancel. All these features are memorials to the Pryse family. From the village the fine mountain road to Pont Erwyd skirts two lakes among forestry plantations.

Trefilan (8). The rather nondescript village is at *Talsarn* on the river Aeron. The pretty little church and even prettier Regency rectory with wide eaves under a hipped slate roof lies off the B.4337 road to Aberystwyth. It was completely rebuilt in 1880 in R. J. Withers' usual style. Further north a lane to the left, signposted *Hermon,* passes an early Methodist chapel hardly bigger than the cottage which it adjoins. The country is very broken here, and north again there are wide views from *Trichrug,* the highest point in the district.

Tregaron (6). This ancient market town, sedate, contained and largely untroubled by traffic or development has preserved, as so many of the smaller Welsh country towns have done, its character and charm. Little has changed in the last 50 years, although only occasionally now is there a whiff of peat fires from the primly curtained houses, and pony trekkers in the central square replace the farmers and their sons, who have given up their Welsh cobs for Land Rovers. Two early 20th-century concrete and iron balustraded bridges span the river *Berwyn* which divides

the town, and across the Square a First World War Memorial Hall of solid respectable design faces the comfortable and attractive *Talbot Hotel,* 19th century and three storeyed in its centre section with sash windows, bracketed eaves, a homespun portico, and low wings on either side. Between, in the open space among the cars and ponies, is the 1893 bronze statue by Albert Toft of Henry Richard (1812–1888), Liberal M.P. for Merthyr. Richard has been called the Apostle of Peace through his advocacy of arbitration as a way of settling international quarrels. Secretary of the Peace Society, he attended congresses all over Europe; in 1873 Parliament passed his motion in favour of international arbitration, and in 1880 a modified motion for gradual and mutual disarmament. He was also a bitter opponent of the partnership of Church and State, and a firm advocate of Welsh Church Disestablishment.

The parish church of St Caron, a stone 14th-century building, has a massive battlemented tower, and the nave and chancel were extensively restored in 1878. It has 20th-century stained glass (Shrigley and Hunt, Lancaster, and Celtic Studios) and an impressive wrought-iron chancel screen. An ancient tablet on the high sloping sill of the tower window cannot be read, but outside the tombstones are worth noting.

The town owes much to its setting; to the east the sheltering foothills of Plinlimon have the velvety green colour of alpine meadows, and to the south and west the Vale of Teifi is richly pastured. Northward the B.4343 road to Devil's Bridge skirts the great bog of Tregaron. Perhaps the best view of the valley is from the lane running above Afon Groes past small farms where pony trekkers stay, a sad deserted Victorian chapel, and on to the Youth Hostel. The best known road is the old drovers' trail over the mountains to the English markets via *Abergwesin,* metalled now but still narrow, and signposted as the Mountain Road.

above and below Llyn Teifi, PONTRHYDFENDIGAID

68

TROEDYRAUR lychgate

heather of the raised bog and Kites and the odd Merlin can be seen in the area. Polecats come down to the bog at night and in summer. The Reserve cannot be entered without a permit, which can be got from the Nature Conservancy, Plâs Gogerddan, Bow Street, Aberystwyth, or from the Assistant Regional Officer Ty Coed, Tregaron.

Troedyraur (7). A scattered upland parish rising steeply from the Ceri valley. The main hamlets are at *Hawen* where is a simple white-washed Congregational Chapel, 1747 and later, with round-headed doors and windows under chocolate coloured arches, and at *Rhydlewis* where Caradoc Evans, early 20th-century satirist of Welsh village life, spent his early years. The church of St Michael on the crossroad above *Brongest* was rebuilt in 1845. It has a classical lychgate with slate flags and good wrought iron gates, and 18th-century memorials surprisingly elegant for the district by T. King, Bath, and D. Mainwaring, Carmarthen, including one to John Lloyd Williams (1745–1838), Senior Fellow of the Royal Society. His contributions to the Society's *Transactions* concerned the making of ice in Benares. The pink and gold plaster mouldings behind the altar and the chocolate coloured wooden bars and frames of the Early English style windows are very Welsh, and it is a pity that even the stonework of the medieval font is hidden under white paint. *Plâs Gwernant,* the only house of any size left in the parish, is now a ruin. It is in a rough classical style of the early 1800s, with a central pediment and two long, two-storeyed wings.

Upper Vaenor (2). A small civil parish, an eastern suburb of Aberystwyth.

Verwick (7). From the northern outskirts of Cardigan the road to Gwbert dips to the level of the estuary where the sand dunes are cluttered with beach huts and caravans among the gorse; then it rises to the bungalow development of *Gwbert* where a large gabled hotel overlooks the estuary and the northern headlands of Pembrokeshire.

It passes through wild, ravine-scored moorland, the Great Desert of Wales, over the river Towy some ten miles from Tregaron. On a darkening evening with the mists rising from the valleys and cloud coming low from the hills, the miles can seem the longest in Wales. About five miles out of Tregaron and beyond the ghostly, peaty *Berwyn Lake,* a lane branches right at *Ffrwyd y Camddwr* and three miles on in Llanddewi Brefi parish is *Soar a Mynydd* Methodist chapel and schoolhouse, perhaps the loneliest place of worship in Great Britain, a primitive 19th-century building among pine and beech trees, with a farmhouse at the back and streams alongside, cascading into the Camddwr.

Cors Tregaron (Tregaron Bog) covers about two thousand acres, and, although part of the Lisburne Estate, is managed by the Nature Conservancy as a National Nature Reserve; the Reserve includes one of Britain's best developed and best preserved raised bogs, and originated from a moraine dammed lake of which all that is left is the river Teifi running through its centre. The lower terraces of the river are grazed but the true bog has no agricultural value. Its interest to naturalists lies in its variety of bog plants of which the rarest is the Royal Fern, and in its bird life. One hundred and fifty three species of birds have been seen up to mid 1970. Rarer and more occasional breeders are Montagu's Harriers, Quail and Corncrakes. Wintering birds include Hen Harriers, Hooper Swans and occasionally Bewick's Swans and Great Grey Shrikes. Since 1967 Greenland White Fronted Geese, which once wintered here in large numbers, have been rare due, it seems, to disturbance by low-flying aircraft, and, despite a fairly effective ban on these, there is as yet no sign that the geese will return. A few Red and Black Grouse breed in the

Eglwys Fach, YSGUBOR Y COED

Inland in a bare treeless countryside, the village is a motley, untidy collection of buildings and corrugated iron. Its hillside church of St Pedrog is dominated by a massive and crumbling west tower whose small, perpendicular windows suggest the 15th century. The rest of the church is a typical mid 19th-century nave and chancel building (architect H. Woodyer), raised above the ordinary by its detail, slate steps to the pulpit, and mid 19th-century stained glass of deep colour by Clayton and Bell in the east window. The tombstones here and those of plain *Siloam* chapel (1796–1831) below are mainly of local slate with well cut lettering and emblems, many of them to local schooner masters. To the west at *Login* is a good chapel and vestry group, the chapel a neat gable of grey dressed stones under a slate roof rebuilt in 1837, with an elegant name plaque, and Welsh inscription in black and silver, and traditional

windows. The whitewashed vestry has granary steps, and a large burial ground is hedged with cypress.

Summer visitors flock to the close cropped downland above *Mwnt Beach,* where a stream falls steeply over outcrops of slate to the yellow sands. Through the cliffs there is a good view of grassy *Cardigan Island* and the blue-grey slate of the cliffs mirror the changing colours of the sea below. On the downland, cropped bare by sheep, a small primitive church, low and starkly whitewashed, lies within a rectangular embankment. Inside, a plain medieval braced roof, rood loft stairs and pieces of carved rood loft timbers, two-light Perpendicular windows at east end and square latticed windows elsewhere. Only discordant note is modern polished slate and gold in the sanctuary. The whole scene is one of special beauty, barely marred by man and his necessities. Tradition sites here a famous victory over

marauding pirates. Another victory was won lately when the Planning Authority refused permission for "development". Attractive modern village school in stone and slate at *Tremain* on the main coast road.

Ysgubor y Coed (3). The most northern parish of the county, with a strong feel of north Wales. A high escarpment of barren land, pierced by the Einion valley, rises to the east of the main road and, to the west, the flat land bordering the Dovey estuary is picturesquely broken by wooded knolls. The Einion meets the plain at *Furnace* in a cascade. The hamlet takes its name from the days of lead ore smelting; the great, thirty-feet-high, iron water wheel which drove the machinery is still in position against the early 19th-century, stone-built, smelting house. When the lead mines gave out it was used for milling and is now derelict.

A little to the north in the hamlet

"Salem", a painting by S. C. Vosper. The setting is Salem Baptist Chapel, Llanbedr, Merioneth, see p. 115.

of *Eglwys Fach,* the path through an early 19th-century lychgate with low, lean-to sheds on each side leads to the pre-Victorian church of St Michael, rebuilt in 1833. The canted east end was added in 1913. It retains many of its original features; low box pews with doors, west gallery with bench seats, Commandments,

Derelict lead mines at
Pontrhydygroes, YSPYTTY YSTWYTH

Creed, and Lord's Prayer boards gold-lettered on the north wall, slate flags and long, pointed diamond paned windows. The plain font in a railed enclosure is probably 13th century. There are tall yew trees in the churchyard. R. S. Thomas, whose poems, many to do with life in the hard uplands of the parish, are in modern anthologies, held the living before his recent move to north Wales.

The principal house, *Glandyfi Castle,* is on the site of the stronghold of the 12th-century Welsh prince Rhys ap Dafydd. The Jeffreys family, one of whom was the Judge of the Bloody Assize, owned the estate for close on three hundred years. The Castle is on a rocky plateau overlooking the Dovey estuary. Now mainly a late 18th-century building externally, with battlemented parapets and round and square tur-

Village memorials: The Rev. Daniel Rowlands, LLANGEITHO. T. E. Ellis, BALA. Henry Richard, TREGARON.

rets, parts of it are Tudor and earlier. It is a house of elegance and distinction. The gardens are usually open to the public for two days in early May. They are admirably landscaped to the rocky slopes shaded by tall beech, oak and Douglas fir, whose upper roots protrude above the rocky soil. Chusan palms from North Asia and flowering shrubs are a feature.

From Glandyfi station yard there is a view across the river of tree-covered *Tomen Las,* a Norman motte with a boathouse; a haunt of herons, ravens and shelducks.

Yspytty Cynfyn *see* **Cwmrheidol.**

Yspytty Ystwyth (6). A parish mainly of mountain and moorland. The only centre of population is at *Pontrhydygroes,* once a prosperous lead mining village, still spick and span in its valley setting. Southward on a windy hill, the 1879 towered church of St John the Baptist was designed by R. J. Withers. Its spacious interior remains as he left it, except for the damp and the ivy creeping through the windows.

Ystrad Meurig (6). In the extreme

south of the parish of *Gwnnws Issa* the village is famous in Wales for its Grammar School, now the College of St John, founded and endowed in the mid 18th century by Edward Richard (1714–1777), son of the local innkeeper and a schoolmaster all his adult life. John Williams (1792–1858), one of the great classical scholars of Wales and first Rector of Edinburgh Academy, was a pupil here. Sir Walter Scott, who helped to found Edinburgh Academy, described him as the best schoolmaster in Europe and with him as inspiration wrote

74

War Memorials: LLANGEITHO, LLANDDEWI BREFI, PONTRHYDFENDIGAID

his Welsh romance *The Betrothed*.

The College has maintained its association with the Church, and a reputation for a sound classical education bringing the disciplines of Latin and Greek to the natural turbulence of Celtic thought and expression. Now an unpretentious whitewashed building almost entirely 19th century, it is a symbol such as is often repeated in Wales of the intellectual struggle to rise above material hardships.

Adjoining the school with pleasant cottages and farmsteads dotted singly around, the church of St John the Baptist was completely rebuilt in Perpendicular style in 1899. Architects, Baker and Hughes. It has pink sandstone arches to chancel, windows and doorways, whitewashed walls, grained pews and clear glass in square panes under a dark panelled roof. 1963 stained glass (J. Wippell, Exeter) in the five-light east window in memory of a former vicar, John Jones, shows incidents in the life of Christ and a modern schoolroom scene. To the north-east *Llanwnnws* church of St Gwnnws stands high among remote lanes, solitary, looking friendless, and locked. Its chancel and nave were rebuilt in 1829 and restored in 1895. A slate roof has replaced the spire of the ancient tower in the south-west corner and an inscribed, cross-incised stone stands in the stone flagged porch. In the north of the parish the plantations of *Mynnyd Bach* slope down to the Ystwyth valley. The 1869 Methodist chapel at *Ty'n y graig* has a pretty, grey gabled front.

Merioneth: **Introduction**

Meirion was a grandson of Cunedda whom the Romans transplanted with his tribe to north Wales about 400 A.D., from Berwick upon Tweed. Cunedda's eight sons established tribal kingdoms as far south as Cardiganshire. The Dovey estuary became the boundary between the northern kingdom of Gwynedd, now the whole of north Wales, and the kingdom of Deheubarth, now the counties of Cardigan, Carmarthen and Pembroke. When Edward I completed the subjugation of the country and tightened his grip on

opposite Craig-yr-Aderyn (Birds Rock) from Castel-y-bere.
opposite below Birds Rock in the Dysynni valley looking towards Castel-y-bere.

Snowdonia, the natural fortress, with an arc of sea-based castles from Rhuddlan in the east to Harlech in the west, Gwynedd was split into shires, of which Merioneth became one. The rebellion of Owain Glyndwr (Shakespeare's Glendower) a native of east Merioneth, united north and south Wales for a brief period in the early part of the 15th century.

Surprisingly, remains of pre-history are scanty. A few dolmen burial chambers (two, close together, easily accessible from the main road at Dyffryn Ardudwy in Llanendwyn parish) are of the Neolithic Age. Bronze Age cairns are scattered on the east-facing slopes of the coastal

below Tomen-y-mur, MAENTWROG. Roman Amphitheatre and mound; the remains of a fortress

mountains and along the ancient trade routes to Ireland from Wessex and northern and eastern Britain. The main routes to the coast followed the valleys of the Dovey and the Dee. Where they traversed high ground and moorland, as for example to Harlech from the Dee near Bala via Cwm Moch and Afon Lliw, they are marked by standing stones and circles as well as by hoards of weapons and implements. There are Iron Age forts along the coast at Pen Dinas (Llanaber) Moel Goedog (north east of Harlech), further inland at Craig y Dinas (due east of the Dyffryn Ardudwy) and at the eastern end of the county at Caer Drewyn (north of Corwen). The Romans, too, trod lightly here and there is little above ground to mark their three camps at Tomen y Mur on their Sarn Helen south-to-north route near Trawsfynydd, at Cefn Caer guarding the Dovey estuary and at Caergai in the Bala valley.

The oldest rocks are in the great Harlech Dome, half ringed on the east and south by the volcanic, igneous rocks of the Arenig, Rhobell and Cader Idris ranges, with Ffestiniog on the south eastern limb of the Snowdonia syncline to the north. The Dome, made up of sediment hardened into grits and conglomerates of sandstone, was deposited in the Cambrian age five hundred million years ago. For the rest of the county, the rocks are mainly beds of shale and slate deposited as sediment in the Ordovician age, one hundred million years later. The slate areas are Blaenau Ffestiniog, and between Towyn and Dinas Mawddwy, principally at Abergynolwyn, Corris and Aberllefeni. The Bala Fault, a great fissure in the earth's crust, runs from Bala Lake westward to beyond Talyllyn Lake. Gold and

Slate fences near BLAENAU FFESTINIOG

copper have been mined around Bontddu in Llanaber parish above the northern bank of the Mawddach estuary and in Llanfachreth parish. Plans are afoot to re-open some of the workings. Manganese has been mined in the shales south and north-west of Y Llethr in the Rhinog range. Below the waters of Cardigan Bay lies a bed of sedimentary rocks reckoned to be between three and four miles thick. The Institute of Geological Sciences, which is responsible for Britain's geological survey, is exploring this bed with a drilling rig erected on Mochras peninsula in Llanenddwyn parish. This is part of a seismic survey programme which has been running for some years in these waters.

Slate has done more to transform the visage of north Wales than anything else. Folded by intense pressures in the earth's crust, a product originally of successive deposits, it has developed the characteristic known as cleavage; it splits into thin, strong layers at angles different from the original strata lines along which other bedded rocks can normally only be split. In the greater Caernarvonshire beds slate is quarried in the open, but in Merioneth it has to be mined from underground chambers, in places over a thousand feet below the surface, because of the overlying beds of hard rock. The industry developed rapidly through the 19th century with an increasing home and export market for roofing slates, reaching its heyday about 1900. Thereafter it declined rapidly, unable to compete with such alternatives as manufactured tiles. Evidence of the important part it has played on land and sea in the life of the people is apparent in the fabric of buildings, the terraced houses of the mining centres, the narrow-gauge railways to the coast, tombstones, and fences against cattle. Only one-tenth and in some mines as little as one-twentieth of the output can be converted into a marketable product, hence the huge heaps of waste material.

The county, roughly triangular, extends from Cardigan Bay across Wales to a point beyond

Pistyll y Cain (*above*) and
Rhaiadr Mawddach, LLANFACHRETH

Bala Lake (Llyn Tegid)

Corwen, about twelve miles from the English border. It has altogether only thirty-nine parishes, many of them areas of barren moor and mountain and one, Llanfor, straddles the county from north to south. It could be said that it has the best scenery in Wales. There are higher mountain peaks in Caernarvonshire and a remoter, fiercer, seaboard in Pembrokeshire; the Vales of Glamorgan and Denbigh are more richly pastured. But Merioneth has the wide estuaries of the Dovey and Mawddach, and Cader Idris; the lonely tarns high in the Rhinogs, Hywel, Pryved, Twr Glas; the lake-embellished Cwm Bychan; the rich woodlands of Ffestiniog and pastures of Dysynni, the Vale of Edeyrnion; the romantic twin waterfalls Pistyll y Cain and Rhaiadr Mawddach, and the high pass between the Arans into the Montgomeryshire plain. No other single county in Wales has such a profusion.

The river Dee, Dyfrdwy in Welsh and sacred in Celtic religion, flowing eastward through Bala Lake (Llyn Tegid) down the Vale of Edeyrnion makes a landscape connection between the eastern part of Merioneth and Denbighshire, to which there is also easy access through Gwyddelwern parish into the Vale of Clwyd. The Vale of Edeyrnion widens around Corwen to form a plain of rich pasture and woodland, the northern and western hills forming a far horizon. But as the Dee bends eastward the hills close in again and the Berwyns dominate the southern flank.

West of Bala the character changes. The

81

rounded hills with their pasture farms "green to the very door" gradually give place to the contorted volcanic peaks and masses of Arenig, Rhobell and Cader in the Aran range. Beyond them is the coastal plain, sometimes narrow, occasionally marshy. From the west the panorama of the mountains best unfolds itself, and unless you are out at sea, there is no better place to stand than on the Mochras peninsula, south of Harlech. As Richard Wilson's painting of Cader Idris condenses into one scene the grandeur of the whole, Hilaire Belloc in one of his less exuberant books, *The Cruise of the Non*, depicts a larger canvas and conveys the emotional appeal. "We cast anchor," he wrote, "in the midst of that solemn bay with its half circle of huge mountains looking down upon an empty sea. . . . There is no corner of Europe that I know, not even the splendid amphitheatre around Udine, which so moves me with the awe and majesty of great things as does this mass of the northern Welsh mountains seen from this corner of the silent sea . . . this awful parade of the great mountains standing on guard over the northern corner of Cardigan Bay, seen from the silence and the flat of the ocean, towering above its glass; and all that late afternoon and evening I adored them."

In the north, beyond the vale of Ffestiniog, the Moelwyns (the Cnicht ridge is part of the county boundary) are an introduction to Snowdonia. The views from the Moelwyn ridge are splendid. Moel Siabod to the right is a lovely pyramid, an extension of the Moelwyn range. The eye is drawn westward past the twin faces of Glydr to the peak of Snowdon, Y Wddfa, from which other crests or cribau radiate, barely lower but low enough to invest Y Wddfa with, one cannot escape the word, its majesty.

Walking in the high hills of Merioneth the senses are assailed as sharply as in Snowdonia, or the English Lake District. Cader Idris, the Arenigs and the Rhinogs all provide the small, classical experiences—the smell of damp moss, and the boggy places that you are on before you can see them; the sheep tracks that seem so errant and vague, and yet add up to the shortest

and, on the whole, the driest route to wherever it is you are going; the white-rumped wheatears darting from rock to rock in front of you; the brace of grouse that suddenly breaks cover at your feet or the resentful croak of a raven that breaks the silence; the half supercilious, half-startled look of the sheep; the variety and closely integrated patterns of the short grass; the gnarled ancient look of the heather branches and their tough resistance to your step; the no-coloured and every-coloured rocks—purple, grey, beige, fawn, umber, sienna, green, mauve, blue—all lost in the pervading green and brown and purple of grass and heather, till you are suddenly upon them. Their shape is so haphazard and so untidy as you approach them that when they come into close view it is astounding to find them assuming the grand, austere, simplified and unhaphazard forms of modern sculpture—great slanted anvils, half-submerged, Brancusi-like fish and birds, big rectangular blocks that are as smooth and polished as a small shore pebble, or as pitted and scored as a bomb-blasted house. They can have striking personalities that take on benevolent or sinister characters according to weather and season, and the feelings of the viewer. Visual sensations can be oddly heightened and distorted. Sudden patches of bleached grass make the immediate surroundings look like a distant landscape with the sun shining in patches; a close rock can echo exactly the form of a distant mountain; the careful, geometrical-looking form of suddenly-disclosed sheep-folds can look like strange works of nature, not of man, while giant groups of rocks that have weathered into basic geometrical schemes seem man-made, not natural.

Some variation in the sky suits these areas best. A set fair sky of unbroken blue makes it lack scale and drama. Richard Wilson's favourite sky—purplish grey clouds with golden edges, and a thin pale blue beyond—these are the best and the most frequent of all.

above Cader Idris from the lower
slopes of Rhinog Fach
below Llyn Du on Rhinog Fawr

River valleys divide these great land masses, and silts from them have caused wide estuaries. The beautiful Vale of Ffestiniog, through Maentwrog, is of rich woodland, banked with flowering shrubs; the Wnion valley from Bala Lake to the Mawddach estuary is confined within the bordering hills until it opens out near Dolgellau. The Dysynni valley is a broad plain of drained marsh and pasture land, barely rising above sea level after it has emerged from the western flank of Cader Idris; not a traffic route, it is quiet, and, around Llanfihangel y Pennant, Arcadian in simplicity. The Dovey, rising on Aran Fawddwy, flows into Montgomeryshire, later to widen into the estuary which forms Merioneth's boundary with Cardigan.

Because there is no heavy industry to be served by road transport, traffic is fairly light. Telford's Shrewsbury to Holyhead road, the first publicly-built "improved" road after the privately-built turnpikes, enters the county between Corwen and Llangollen. West of Corwen, it re-enters Denbighshire and a straight road follows the natural fracture line of the Bala Fault to Dolgellau and the coast. From Bala a bare mountain road over-hung with electric cables strikes north to Ffestiniog, landscaped along the Tryweryn reservoir, and skirts the north flank of Arenig Fawr. From Dolgellau the Ffestiniog road emerges from a wooded valley to traverse a treeless plain, Wild-West stage-coach country, from which there are views of the Rhinog peaks, heart of the Harlech Dome— Rocky Mountains in miniature. From the south there is a fast open road branching right at Mallwyd over the southern slopes of the Aran range to high ground above Dolgellau. At Cross Foxes it joins one of the most spectacular roads in Britain which runs along the eastern flank of Cader Idris over a mountain pass. There is a feeling that a sudden explosion has rent the earth's crust and, there, seven hundred feet below in the distance, lies the long, slender Talyllyn.

Flatlands sheltered from the sea by sand dunes alternate with exciting cliff-hanger stretches

Slope of Craig y Pant, Bwlch y Groes

along the coast road from Aberdovey to Harlech. North of Barmouth the lowland is dense with caravan camps but they seem distant enough from the main road—this great tented holiday army. Their unsightliness has to be measured always against the enjoyment and health they provide. The country here is threaded with dry stone walls, which enclose the sheep pastures and border the roads and lanes. They are of rough, rounded boulders, which decrease in size from the bottom upwards.

The roads which follow the estuaries and valleys of the coast can come as a welcome relief from those of the bare highland. They wind sometimes through broken outcrops of rock and stunted oaks, sometimes past great banks of rhododendrons, bordered by hamlets and small country houses which have changed little over the last hundred years. The road from Pennal to Aberdovey along the Dovey estuary is a miniature Corniche; the road from Dolgellau to Barmouth through Bontddu gives views of the estuary and the hazy ridges of Cader Idris.

The towns, little more than market centres and guardians of Welsh habits and 19th-century cultural traditions against the influence of larger, cosmopolitan towns, are "unripe for development" and reasonably well contained; they have that particular Welsh personality, compounded of bric-à-brac architectural oddities, sedateness, and withdrawn, lace-curtained, surface respectability over which the chapels still brood from within their railings. Corwen, a market town and once a staging post on an important trunk route, suffers from its north- and east-facing aspect, backed by the Berwyn range. Bala has cultural associations that run as deep in the life and thought of Wales as the waters of its lake, and Dolgellau, now the county town, owes much to its Tyrolean setting against the backcloth of Cader Idris. Aberdovey, originally a small port, is the best of the coast resorts, small and circumscribed. It has longstanding family associations with England and the outside world. Towyn and

Barmouth, with personalities of their own, have an unfinished look about their sea fronts, due partly to the interruption and after-effects of the Second World War. Harlech, now high above the marsh, has the narrow streets of a medieval settlement under the protection of its castle; a quondam county town dedicated to tourists and golf—and education. The slate-mine town of Blaenau Ffestiniog and the villages of Corris and Abergynolwyn look as if they have been detached from Tonypandy or Pontypridd in the days of the depression; they have the terraces, chapels and Co-operative Stores, the strong industrial personality, the brave face and the pride of a closely-knit community.

Welsh is still the first language of the county, although along the coast, whose mild, sheltered climate attracts English residents, the accents of the Midlands and the North are noticeable. One in three school-leavers seeks employment outside the county.

Harlech Castle is a major architectural monument. Domestic architecture is conditioned by the use of local material; slate or shale laid in horizontal slabs, dark granitic stone and the inevitable blue roof slates. At two country houses in the Vale of Edeyrnion, Rhug and Pale Hall, a cinnamon-coloured, easily worked sandstone from the Cefn quarries, now closed, near Ruabon has been used. Some smaller houses, noticeably in the streets of Dolgellau, are built of rough, rounded boulders, undressed and heavily cemented. Pressed red bricks are little in evidence. As the local material is in the main weatherproof, and as the granite and slate blocks, often very large in size, are so closely dressed, stucco and colour washes are not so prevalent as they are south of the Dovey.

There are a good many 17th-century manors or squires' houses, very much in their original condition after adaptation from earlier cores, and with interior features such as stair-cases, fire-places, panelling and other woodwork, of surprising richness. Some are embellished with armorial emblems and dates, suggesting a period of pride and prosperity in the first half of the century. Rows of dormer windows, gables

and weathered stones and, in one or two places, their free-standing gatehouses, give distinction to the county as similar houses in a softer medium do to the Cotswolds; the richer cattle drovers may have retained mental images of what they saw along their trails through England. This style of architecture is sometimes repeated at a humbler domestic level; it was taken as a model by the Victorians for rows of cottages, for example, at Arthog and Dolgellau. Good examples of the larger houses are Glyn Clywarch, Dolaugwyn (these are two beauties), Caer Berllan, Dolymoch, Plâs Rhiw-waedog, Cynfal Fawr, Maes y Neuadd and the older part of Cors y Gedol. (See index and gazetteer for location and details of these, and other buildings mentioned below.)

The Georgian period is best represented, if sparsely, by Talgarth, Nannau, Plâs Brondanw (rebuilt) Caerynwch, Gwerclas, Rhug and Peniarth. Peniarth charms instantly by its absence of formalism and by its evolution as a lived-in, cherished home. Its brick elevation gives it warmth and character. Strangely, no architect's name is associated with any of these houses. Georgian houses can also be picked out along the sea front at Aberdovey and in the towns.

The Victorians have left their medieval-revival mark in the ramparts of Tanybwlch and Castell Deudraeth, their baronial aspirations in Pale Hall and their Gothic predelictions in Dolmelynllyn and Hengwrt (Llanfachreth) and Tyn y Coed and in the seaside hotels and boarding houses. Jacobean, Georgian or Victorian, these are isolated examples, hardly conferring on the county, except perhaps for the Victorian gables of the seaside towns, a special character or individuality. For that one must look to the humbler farms. In the fabric of these one sees the straight-forward, pragmatic approach of the builders, often pre-17th century. It is at once noticeable how well they marry with the lie of the land, taking advantage of shelter and aspect. Placed so often on rising damp-free ground the buildings have been hewn

HARLECH CASTLE

The Mawddach estuary

into the hillside so that they are in practice of two storeys, the upper one originally the dwelling part and the lower one the byre and stabling. As time has passed, dormer windows have been thrown out of the upper storey and the dwelling-space increased. Anyone living in a stone country becomes aware of the ease and skill with which stones and boulders are moved by leverage and put together to form a wall. Stone-built farms and barns, particularly gable ends, are beautifully made. With large boulders at the base the courses of rough undressed stones, often waterworn and rounded, rise without cement or any form of binding to a well-graded apex. A barn in the farmyard of Mochras has boulders at ground level at least three feet long.

Civic architecture is modest. There are bits of late Georgian in Dolgellau, there is a home-spun but coherent workhouse building in Corwen, also late Georgian, and 20th-century work by Sir Giles Gilbert Scott in the County Offices, Dolgellau, and by Clough Williams Ellis in the Memorial Hospital, Blaenau Ffestiniog. Maentwrog is an example of 1830 model village planning, with buildings of local slate. Portmeirion in its lovely natural setting is—Portmeirion.

Most of the churches are small bellcote chambers, admirably suited to the high ground on which they are usually found. The larger buildings in the towns and valleys, often with towers at the west end, are also characteristically Welsh in their plainness. Bits and pieces of medieval woodwork have survived liturgical purges, or have been salvaged from larger units by Victorian restorers; for instance, what is now the reredos in Bettws Gwerfil Goch. Simple medieval roofs are common. The rood loft and screen of Llanegryn church are among the best in Britain. There is barely a pane of medieval glass. The 13th-century arcades

The Glaslyn estuary

and windows of Llanaber church should delight the medievalist; Llanfrothen, Llangelynin and Llandanwg old church are primitive, and Llangar old church, untouched since the early 18th century, is now being rescued from decay and collapse. Successive owners of the Rhug estates are to be congratulated on having preserved the interior (barely larger than a country house dining room) of their private chapel as a most extraordinary exhibition of Jacobean Baroque, late, almost last medieval, and emergent Classical.

Rebuilding in the late Classical and preaching-house tradition prior to the Gothic revival has produced early 19th-century churches at Dolgellau (nave), Pennal, Aberdovey, Barmouth (St Davids), Llwyngwril, Blaenau Ffestiniog and Harlech but most of them have been brought into the later Victorian fashion by east-end extensions and Gothicised windows and doors.

Benjamin Ferrey seems to have been the favourite Victorian architect and restorer in the county; his most imposing church is in Bala. St Philip's (Caerdeon) in Llanaber parish, and privately built, is modelled on a Basque village church and in these similar surroundings looks very well. It has an exterior colonnade of the kind in which Basque village elders hold their council meetings. But as time passes, and if climate and neglect do not corrupt, the most striking modern church in the county and the most interesting to students and historians of church architecture and furnishing will be St Peter's, Brithdir, by J. P. Sedding and Harry Wilson. Sir Gilbert Scott designed a small church in Llandderfel parish.

Chapel architecture is monotonous; here again the weatherproof fabric removes the need for colour wash, whose variations can be such an exuberant feature of chapels to the south, and

The Manod, near FFESTINIOG

the plain block stone lacks texture and feeling; but there is one eyecatcher on the outskirts of Llandrillo. Also, chapel building does not seem to have got into its stride in these parts until the second half of the 19th century when patterns became more stereotyped anyway. But the Baptist chapel, Salem, in Llanbedr parish has, outside and inside, the simplicity of the pre-revivalist meeting house; so, too, has another Salem in Llangar parish.

Frank Ward's *Lakes of Wales*, an angler's book, is an excellent topographical guide to the many lakes, most of them remote, in the county as in other Welsh counties. *The Life and Opinions of Robert Roberts, Travelling Scholar*, is a remarkable autobiography of mid 19th-century life in north Wales, especially in the Vale of Edeyrnion; particularly interesting in its account of the relations between church and Calvinistic Methodism. Both these books are out of print. The 1916 *Royal Commission Report on Ancient Monuments* in the county is sketchy and not very good. Better is the *History of Merioneth*, in two volumes, by Dr E. G. Bowen and C. A. Gresham, published by the Merioneth Historical and Record Society, Dolgellau. The first volume, which has appeared, carries the history of the county up to the Age of the Native Princes.

N.B.—Llwybr Cyhoeddus on signposts means Public Footpath.

92

Merioneth: **Gazetteer**

The number after each entry refers to the square on the map of Merioneth where the place is to be found

Aberdovey (7). The Cote d'Azur, Biarritz, Aberdovey—all reflect the late Victorian and Edwardian flair of the English for establishing colonies at choice points on the shores of their neighbours. Aberdovey developed from a small port into a coastal resort. Narrow central lanes, a waterside warehouse and a wooden jetty recall the days when ships unloaded timber and coal and left with cargoes of slate. The English influence can be seen in the trim hillside villas, with flowering shrubs, which thrive in this mild and sheltered climate, and in the eighteen-hole golf course, of championship standard, among the dunes west of the village. It was laid out between 1886 and 1892 and Bernard Darwin, its Life President, wrote lovingly of it. Development, restricted on the east side by the steeply rising ground, now tends towards Towyn. At each end there is an Outward Bound School, girls at the west and boys at the east. Along part of the sea front high tide reaches the embankment, but west of the jetty a low bank of dunes intervenes, dotted with wooden bathing huts. The buildings along the sea front, sometimes almost built into the high rock, have architectural interest and charm: there are Victorian gabled and bay windowed houses and shops of varying elevation, a late 18th-century hotel, *The Dovey,* a massive parish church of horizontal slate slabs, and some elegant late Georgian town houses. The Dovey, formerly the Ship Inn, has a plaque to say that it was built by Athelstane Owen in 1792. Its high, six-light rectangular bay windows and central window under a moulded architrave, all picked out in black against a white background, make a striking façade. The parish church of St Peter was built in 1837, with a west tower and gallery. The latter was removed in a later restoration, when the chancel was added and the windows given the medieval look. The panelled nave ceiling re-

ARAN MAWDDWY

mains, though now marred by hanging chromium heaters. So do the Lord's Prayer, Creed and Commandment boards. A brass tablet, by Peter Morton, has a portrait in judge's robes of Baron James Richard Atkin (1857–1944), Lord of Appeal, who helped to draw up the Constitution of the Church in Wales after its severance from the State by the Disestablishment Act. The belfry has a peal of ten bells, but the bells of the song are supposed to sound from below the waters of the estuary.

Aran (5). A range which carries the line of the Berwyn hills westward along the southern part of the county, falling as much as two thousand feet into the cleft running down to Talyllyn lake, then to rise again to its former height on the great escarpment of Cader Idris. Of the Arans

proper *Mawddwy* at two thousand nine hundred and seventy feet is the highest peak in Wales outside the Snowdonia range. With its neighbour *Benllyn,* some seventy feet lower, to which it is connected by a mile-long ridge it forms a bare desolate expanse scored by water courses on its western slopes and a steep scarp on the eastern side. Two ways to the ridge are suggested. The first is by way of Dinas Mawddwy and up the Cowarch valley to where the mountains close in and the narrow lane finishes, opposite the farm of *Cae Peris.* Here the sight of the towering, rocky peaks is enough to daunt anyone; but the ascent, starting by the footpath opposite Cae Peris and across the stream is easy enough once the first steep incline has been climbed and open country reached. The path easily follows the flank of the rushy

hills on the east side of Hengwm valley, past sheep dips and pens of corrugated iron and quartz-veined stones. As the path rises, the stream in the valley below shrinks to a narrow thread, losing its own identity on a flat stretch of grass and stones, where rivulets from the enclosing hills meet to form its source. The opposite slopes are thick with bracken, whose regular pattern is broken in places by barer patches, assuming strange shapes, sometimes angular and sometimes horse-shoe. But when you walk on the eastern slope, the going is easy enough though boggy in places and with a steep drop to the valley. The way lies over the rugged narrow pass of Drws Bach (little door) and so to the

ARAN BENLLYN

94

triangulation mark. The views are immense—Plinlimon and the Desert of Wales to the south-west, the Shropshire Housman land to the east.

The other ascent is from the Wnion valley between Bala and Dolgellau, and the starting place is either the farm of *Dolddeuli,* less than a mile north-east of Drws y Nant station or Pant Clyd, nearer Bala. There is a good Forestry Commission road (cars by permission) from Dolddeuli, snaking up the hillside; towards the top, a branch to the right which seems to go down hill in fact climbs to the highest part of the forest at Pared yr Ychain on or about the sixteen hundred foot contour line. There is a short scramble through the conifers along a stream to the open, and then a stiff climb gradually easing, up the brow of Aran Fawddwy. The Forestry road is relatively good, but at intervals stretches of loose jagged stones could be harmful. The route from Pant Clyd, clear from the Ordnance Survey map, is less direct but it avoids the steep climb from Pared yr Ychain.

Arenig (2). Fawr and Fach (big and little), mountains on the south and north side respectively of the Bala to Ffestiniog (B.4391) road. At two thousand eight hundred feet *Fawr* is the higher by some five hundred feet, a massive table-land conical at its highest point. The ascent, though not difficult, looks easier than it is from the usual starting point at the ruins of a farmhouse between the granite quarry and the bridge at *Rhydyfen.* At first it is steep enough, then levelling off past a cluster of sheep pens, boulder walled, whose outlines suggest those of a chambered prehistoric site. Across the plateau a distant saddle ridge between *Craig yr Hyrddod* on the right and a rocky bluff on the left suggests that the peak is near; wrongly, it is not even in sight. Off to the left, a line of boundary fencing leads upwards, the way to it broken by outcrops of grey, weathered stone in patterns, layers and pockets which would delight a rock garden enthusiast.

above ARENIGS from Bwlch y Groes
below Llyn Arenig Fawr

Eventually the peak is in sight, often in mist; from it a panorama opens, broken, and its interest enlivened, by the many lakes glittering in the distance. Beside the triangulation mark is a shallow man-made bowl of roughly heaped stones containing pieces of wreckage of a US Flying Fortress, which crashed on the Arenig, on 4 August, 1943. A slate tablet records the event, with the names and homes of the eight members of the crew who lost their lives, from Idaho, Illinois, Kentucky, New York, Ohio, California, Michigan, Pennsylvania.

If you are minded to return via the lake at the north-eastern foot of the mountain, you should strike northwards along the ridge following the stone cairns. The descent is easy enough, and whether or not you wish to stand on the lake shore, you should follow the downward course of the stream which enters the lake at its south-western edge. Do not be tempted, having seen the lake, to take a short cut back to base along the upper flank of *Gelli Deg.* You could be in trouble among the deep heather, boulders and cliff faces.

Arenig Fach is a much tamer mountain; the route to the top is evident enough from the opposite slopes; the ground slopes gently to Y Foel at about seventeen hundred feet, and then the way lies through heather and rocks to the top.

J. D. Innes, Derwent Lees and the young Augustus John painted the Arenigs in the early years of this century.

Arthog *see* **Llangelynin.**

Bala (2). Lakeside, Calvinist town; a Welsh Geneva. Thomas Charles (1755–1814), ordained in the Established Church, broke away from it in despair in 1811, and was the force behind the spread of Calvinistic Methodism, or Presbyterianism, throughout Wales. He lived where Barclays Bank now stands. In 1837 Dr Lewis Edwards founded a college for young preachers in that faith, and the building in the Gothic Collegiate style of the 1860s with a prominent central tower on its hillside site dominates the northern approach to the town. It is now being adapted to a Welsh Presbyterian Youth Centre.

The richness of the surrounding agricultural land and the attraction of the lake give Bala local distinction. It has the usual character of Welsh country towns, with a medley of bric-à-brac architecture from the 18th century onward, none of it having any particular merit but combining to form an agreeable whole, and give the impression that life could be pleasant enough in such surroundings. Plain Georgian sash windowed fronts alternate with Victorian gables and bay windows, stucco with stone and banker's red brick. Where stone shows, it has a soft and pleasant, grey rainwashed look, well observed in the stationer's corner shop opposite the White Lion Hotel. There is uniformity only in the slate of the roofs.

In the summer holiday season, particularly at weekends, the town seems to burst at its single seam, Stryd Fawr or the long High Street, which stretches from the bridge over the Tryweryn river on the east almost to the shore of the lake. All the business of the town is along this street, all the coastwise and returning traffic. Among the shops, banks and hotels (chapels are little in evidence) milk bar and salon signs and fronts against earlier and more sedate backgrounds give spice and little offence; there are as yet no stretches of plate glass or signs of external interference. It is best to park on the wide tree-lined street and walk around. At the northern end behind the now disused Grammar School (founded in 1713 by Edmund Meyrick and rebuilt in 1851 by Jesus College, Oxford) *Tomen y Bala,* probably a Norman mound, tree-capped, is slighted by public lavatories in the foreground. A little way up the High Street, the 18th-century English Presbyterian chapel, once the town church, is an unusual central pinnacle of dark stone with narrow aisles on each side, pitch-piney inside, with rush chairs. In the High Street proper, the statue of T. E. Ellis (1859–1899), Chief Liberal Whip, dominates and with outstretched arm tries to control the bustle around. Nearby, *Heulwen* is a pretty little private house with cast iron balcony. The best building, and homespun enough at that, is the Town Hall, originally the market

97

hall. It is square Georgian with well spaced windows, round-headed on the ground floor. An 1868 clock tower rises from a hipped roof. Opposite, the *White Lion Hotel* carries the date 1759 and has been considerably enlarged in the 19th century, and since. Down Tegid Street (the side streets are dull and narrow), the white marble 1875 statue of Thomas Charles stands in front of the Welsh Presbyterian chapel making a harmonious whole. The chapel is late Victorian with an end spire, all in light grey stone, and a well carved rosette above the central arch adds character. Christ-church (1855, architect E. B. Ferrey) is an imposing town church with a tall spire, lofty nave and narrow aisles, on the edge of the modern school and playing fields below the

College (Bala is in the ecclesiastical parish of Llanycil).

Llyn Tegid, or Bala Lake, most of which is outside Bala parish, is four and a half miles long and at its widest one mile across. There is a rare species of fish, locally called Gwyniad, not unlike a dace and averaging half a pound in weight. There is no record of one having been caught on rod or line. The lake has an active sailing club and motor boats are prohibited. There is a fine lakeside road along its northern shore, and, around, are the broken skyline of majestic mountains, Cader Idris dimly outlined in the far south-west. The town and the surrounding countryside were formerly famous for the quality of their homespun flannel stockings. George III would wear none other.

Barmouth (4). The older part of this seaside town rises by steep footpaths and steps, which wind and twist through a maze of grey stone cottages and terraces; a town planner's nightmare, yet the houses are so sited that none seems to overlook another. It has been compared with Clovelly but the whole in a different colour might be a north African Kasbah or a Moorish village in southern Spain. Nine of the cottages, including *Rock Terrace,* were given by Mrs Talbot, a local resident, to form part of Ruskin's Guild of St George and are administered by the Ruskin Trust, founded in 1871.

At sea level there is a salty tang around the harbour and its fishing craft; otherwise, the town, virtually one long High Street running parallel to an even longer sea promenade, is

laid out to cater for summer visitors attracted by the splendid, golden sands. There is the usual array of gabled and bay windowed boarding houses, all Victorian and later. The predominant colour is that of the light grey local stone, relieved occasionally by a locally quarried greenish sandstone, as in the gabled façade of 1856 *Ebenezer* Methodist chapel in High Street and in the 1830 Welsh Church of St David, near the harbour. Designed by E. Haycock of Shrewsbury as a single chamber building with short transepts, the latter was touched up and repaired in 1887. The Welsh leaning towards decoration is shown in the cream pews, pale blue ceiling, pinkish cream walls; even the organ pipes are painted in differing pastel shades. Stained 1870-ish glass in the three-

light east window by Alexander Gibbs of Bedford Square.

The parish church of St John the Evangelist is a much more impressive building, of dark grey stone relieved by red sandstone door and window dressings. Built in 1889 (architects Douglas and Fordham, Chester—hence the red sandstone), it has a massive east end tower and the interior is vast by Welsh standards. Sandstone arcades of five bays separate the nave from the aisles, and clerestory windows give extra light. Kempe style stained glass. A scallop shell in the outstretched hand of a kneeling angel, all in marble, serves as a font. Art Nouveau suggestion about the lectern.

Isolated, and on waste ground north of the harbour, stands a small round stone building, erected in the

1820s to impound roistering sailors, and miners from the Bontddu gold workings. It had separate female accommodation. It now houses building materials and on washing days clothes lines connect it with the backs of neighbouring houses. There's talk of turning it into a small museum. Let us hope it will be preserved, even as it is today; it has something pleasantly irreverent about it.

As a whole the town lacks containment, and straggles out into the countryside, necessarily along the coast road. There is a sense that some vitality has gone from it.

Berwyn (3). The southern boundary of the county, north-east of the Arans, lies along the highest ridge of this range. Its slopes, more weathered and rounded by time than

99

the other ranges, are for the most part bracken and grass, except where the forestry plantations following the valley clefts are gradually encroaching on the higher ground. *Cadair Bronwen,* the second highest point, is easily reached on foot from Cadwst, midway between Llandrillo and Pennant (see O.S. 1-inch map). *Cadair Berwyn,* the highest point, lies along the ridge a little way to the south. A longer route, by foot only, is by way of *Ffordd Gam Elin* or Sarn Helen, off the main Llandrillo to Corwen road. Access through the Trystion valley in Llangar parish, though perfectly feasible by car, is not at present recommended. In the extreme north of the county in the parish of Glyndyfrdwy, a lane rises steeply from the main road to Llangollen to the foot of *Moel Fferna* and its disused, underground slate quarries. The Berwyn ridge is excellent walking country with immense views.

Bettws Gwerfil Goch (3). The hamlet which gives this tiny parish its name is a jumble of pretty, unspoilt cottages deep in a hidden valley near the Denbighshire border. The small church of St Mary in a circular churchyard was much restored in 1882 by John Douglas of Chester. It has rough unplastered walls and a medieval roof. Panels from the rood screen now form the reredos; they have 15th-century relief carvings of the Crucifixion, with St John and the Virgin wrongly placed on either side; the outer panels carry emblems of the Passion, hammer, nails, pincer and sword. An 18th-century chandelier of wood with metal branches hangs over the chancel, and there is a brass 18th-century wall tablet to John Maesmor, with verses in Welsh. The pulpit is dated 1741. Modern stained glass by Swaine Bourne, Birmingham, in the church and in the slate-floored porch. Row of tall yew trees outside. In his autobiography Augustus John recounts nocturnal adventures in the village, and encounters with gipsies. South, to the main road, beyond the rising ground, are the spreading oaks and grassy hummocks of Rhug park.

right BRITHDIR: The altar
            by Harry Wilson 1896
opposite Detail

Blaenau Ffestiniog *see* **Ffestiniog.**

Brithdir (5). An enormous parish, of considerable and varied scenic beauty, extending from west of Penmaenpool on the Mawddach estuary to about eight miles east of Dolgellau, its southern boundary the ridge of the Cader Idris range. The eastern part is shown on the O.S. map as Islawr'dref. The main road between Arthog and Penmaenpool is entrancing along its gently winding length; distant views of mountain and estuary are interrupted by closer views of serrated rock outcrops and stunted trees; drives wind to hidden country houses, and pleasant cottages and villas, self assured in stone, grace the roadside verges.

Marshland opens to view at *Penmaenpool,* below the *George III Hotel,* where the estuary is crossed by a wooden toll bridge. Shelldrake nest in the hillside above, and walk their young down well defined and traditional paths and across the main road to the marsh, on which Welsh Black cattle graze. There is a roadside village community at Penmaenpool, a relic of boatyards.

The only other settlement is at *Brithdir,* a scattered village of pretty cottages, off the main Dolgellau Machynlleth road. The only house of any importance in the village is here—*Caerynwch Hall* (not a hotel, as shown on the O.S. map). Built in 1786 in massive blocks of dressed granite and enlarged in 1872, its

south-west elevation can be seen clearly from the main road south of Cross Foxes. Of two storeys and canted bays under wide eaves, it was built for Sir Richard Richards (1752–1823), Lord Chief Baron of the Exchequer Court from 1817. His descendants maintain from Caerynwch the close family association with Dolgellau, where Eldon Square was named after Lord Eldon, Sir Richard Richards' friend. In the grounds of the Hall, *Plâs Hên,* the original family house is a perfect example of the small manor house of the county. Built about 1620, it has a pleasant series of dormer windows and original panelling on the ground floor. Clough Williams Ellis planned a 1921 restoration without in any way altering its outside character.

Church crawlers must not miss St Mark's Church, in an ornamental, summer-house setting of trees and shrubs at the western approach to Brithdir village. It was built in 1896 to the memory of Charles Tooth, chaplain of the then Anglican church of St Mark in Florence, by his widow, a member of the Richards family, and is a replica of the Florence church. Both were designed by J. Sedding and his partner Harry Wilson

and embellished inside in an elaborate art nouveau style. The fabric is of local granite blocks, beautifully dressed and set, under a roof of local Aberllefenni slates, sloping steeply, almost to head level above the south porch. An outside feature is a massive stone cross jutting from the west wall below a rounded hood. The plan is cruciform, with a bellcote above the chancel arch, and a canted east end. Inside, the chancel and sanctuary are dark, dimly lit by natural light, their walls rough cast and painted their original colour of red ochre under a pale blue roof. The beaten copper repoussé fronts of altar, reredos and pulpit are inescapable, and so is the leaden font decorated with foliage and scallops, from the Central School of Design, London (it would be pleasant to think that in using copper and lead, Wilson was conscious of local minerals). The altar front is beaten into a pattern of flowers; on this the Annunciation scene with the figures of the Virgin and the Angel is raised. The reredos is a panel of beaten copper with a vine springing from a chalice and the Latin inscription of *This is the cup of the New Testament in my blood.* Raised patterns

of bluebells spring out of the monogram I.H.S. The pulpit panels carry the text *Now gird up thy loins and say to them the things that deliver thee.* In the centre of each panel is a large circle, a bunch of grapes enclosed in a wreath of leaves. Look also at the carpentry of the doors, flecked very slightly with mother of pearl inlay and at the carved squirrel and hare on the Spanish chestnut choir stalls. Art nouveau flimsy in the carpentry of the north transept gallery and sad indications thereabouts of damp and decay.

While building the church the architect wrote: "The essential condition of real architecture is that the building shall be formed of the materials gathered in the neighbourhood. There is a subtle connection between the look of a scene and the geology of it; the art of the place must be of the place, not imported into it. I have omitted everything like carving or elaborate masonry and rely for effect entirely on the colour of the stone, the method of building and the proportions. Internally I have had in mind one of those delightfully simple churches just south of the Alps where all the effect comes from management of the light and the proportions of the roof and walls. I was tempted to put in columns and mouldings but quite apart from my invincible dislike of any copying of medieval details I felt that the site and nature of the materials forbade any work of that kind"; and again, "I have not given you a church turned out in a mould. I have built it as simply as I know how and have been looking forward to embellishing it in an individual and country manner; the copper work cannot be made by machinery any more than a picture can be so painted"; and, finally, "The church pleased me very much; it all looks as though it had sprung out of the soil, instead of being planted on it". The church was consecrated by the Bishop of Aberdeen, no doubt himself a granite man.

From Cross Foxes a splendid road over the Oerddrws pass falls into the Dovey valley, with near and far views of the bare Aran range.

Cader Idris (7). Cader Idris; the chair of Idris. One will tell you that he was a mythological giant, another that he was a descendant of Cunedda and killed in battle. The mountain has distinctive southern and northern aspects, the southern slopes rise in fairly gentle gradations to the cliffs just below the summit, the northern flank is a great escarpment of granite. A point a little beyond *Llyn Gwernan*, on the side road west from Dolgellau marked Cader Idris gives the best close view of the three main peaks, *Tyrau Mawr* to the far west, *Cyfrwy* (*Saddle*) and *Pen y Gadair* a short distance along the ridge to the east. The resemblance to the back rest of a chair is clear in the concave bow between Cyfrwy and Pen y Gadair. Funnel-shaped screes, like sand flowing in a gigantic hour glass, spill out of the lower crevices of Cyfrwy and on the higher peak a single scar-like scree line, visible from afar, gives precarious foot passage to the summit.

The *Foxes Path* and the *Pony Track* are the two well-known ways of climbing Cader. The former is the most direct route. It starts opposite the *Lake Gwernan Hotel* and soon levels off to gently rising ground as far as the small reeded *Llyn Gafr*. Then the path marked by small heaps of stones rises much more abruptly to *Llyn Gadair*, hidden beyond the ridge. Finally the ascent to the ridge slightly east of the peak is almost vertical, either in the loose scree or up the rocky course of a stream which has its spring near the mountain top. It is not for the faint-hearted, the middle- or over-aged or for those not suitably shod. It is worth going a little down the reverse slope of the ridge for the awe-inspiring view of Llyn Cau.

The Pony Track starting from opposite the car park half a mile or so west by Lake Gwernan is much less arduous to walk, although the distance is much greater. It takes you well to the right of Cyfrwy and strikes the escarpment at its gentlest slope. From then on it is a steady pull eastward, behind Cyfrwy and along the reverse slope of the ridge where a clearly defined path avoids the drifts of large loose rocks which encumber the ground.

Scenically in its immediate surroundings the southern route is much more diverse and interesting. It can best start at the camping site of Doleinion Guest House, where the Machynlleth–Dolgellau road drops into the valley to meet the road to Talyllyn. Invariably, and this is no exception, the path from the valley to the first ridge is almost the steepest part of the journey. Here it passes under pine and oak trees whose shallow protruding roots and the occasional boulder provide natural steps. To the right a waterfall emphasises the steepness of the gradient and through the trees there is a view of steep rocks beyond the water. Flycatchers and wagtails are much in evidence. Soon the tree line is reached and from then on the terrain flattens to give easier walking. There are good close views of the boulder strewn stream. Farther on and to the right the scree mountainside rises almost precipitously and one marvels at the patience and indeed the purpose of the builders of the dry wall which partitions this most barren slope. Beneath a boulder, high on this slope, on *Ystradgwyn*, some two thousand years ago, someone, probably a travelling smith, left eighteen pieces of bronze ware including shield bosses. They lay there until their quite casual discovery in 1963. *Llyn Cau* lies beyond the second of two low ridges which restrict the immediate forward view. Set in a deep crater or chasm and enclosed on three sides by the towering masses of Cader Idris and grassy and swampy on its eastern shore, it owes its fame as much to Richard Wilson's painting of its landscape in the National Gallery as to its own lovely and majestic setting. From the lake you can pick your way to the summit ridge, twelve hundred feet above, preferably choosing a route to the right of the lake.

Never attempt to climb Cader beyond Llyn Gafr on the north or Llyn Cau on the south if there is any mist about. If there is, it can come down suddenly and reduce visibility to a few yards. Locals say that if you have to spend a night on Cader Idris you are turned into a bard or a lunatic.

Corwen (3). Telford's great road, now A.5, to Holyhead, enters the county along the northern flank of the Berwyn range east of *Glyndyfrdwy*, a straggling village with an 1858 bellcote church (St Thomas) by T. H. Wyatt, decent and uncluttered, with slate flags and shallow sanctuary steps and deep red and blue colour in the three-light east window. Two miles or so to the west, *St David's College* (1900-ish), stone built with twin gables and two-storeyed bays on its south elevation, looks well against the northern hills. Built as a private house by the Bouchier family, it is now a Roman Catholic missionary training college.

The Glyndyfrdwy village hall is named after Owain Glyndwr and displays the facsimile of a treaty which he signed with France during his fight against the English for Welsh independence from 1400 to his death in 1415. Glyndwr, knighted by Richard II in return for military service, held much land in the district, some of which was unjustly handed over by Henry IV to a treacherous neighbour, Lord Grey of Ruthin. The whole of Wales rose to support Glyndwr who was finally forced to the role of a guerrilla fighter and disappeared from the scene, no one knows where or how.

Off the secondary road from Carrog to Corwen deep in the shade of oak trees, *Rhagad Hall* is a very pleasant *c.* 1820 stone built country house, added to an earlier farmhouse. It is of two storeys under very wide eaves and the south front has two-storey twin bows with the lower sash windows carried to the floor level. There is a small armorial cartouche of the Lloyd family finely cut in slate over the entrance porch on the east elevation. *Owain Glyndwr's Mount,* between A.5 and the Dee about four miles east of Corwen, is probably the site of a Norman Motte and Bailey castle, and not the burial place of a chieftain.

At Corwen the northern hills recede, leaving an expanse of rich valley land, pastured and royally wooded with oak. The town is a north-facing double chain of buildings, subdued in colour, flanking the

Corris *see* **Talyllyn**.

Llyn Cau, CADER IDRIS

old coach road. To English eyes it is little more than a village, but as a market town it is of service to a wide agricultural community. An open space in the centre is overlooked by the *Owain Glyndwr Hotel,* which has Victorian embellishment. The parish church, dedicated to the Saints Mael and Sulien, broods over a closely tenanted graveyard. It has a plain, low, 13th-century west tower; a restoration in 1870 produced a south aisle with low windows and an arcade of heavy masonry, robbing the interior of light which is further restricted by beige and brown coloured walls; texts and monograms in thick archaic lettering in the chancel and sanctuary add to the gloom. The nave has a massive open roof of richly darkened oak; other medieval features are a huge hollowed-out chest with original iron work, and a heavy circular font with cable moulding at the base. Stained glass is modest and deep mid-Victorian. Tablets are from the 18th century onwards; the best, to the Salesbury family of Rhug, is late 18th century by Vander Hagen of Shrewsbury. Another, later, details the career of Captain Blake, R.N., victim of the Ashanti wars. On the southern boundary of the churchyard, the 18th-century *Old Clergy House* is being modernised internally.

There are no noteworthy chapels and the most striking building is the early 19th-century workhouse, now offices of the Ryder seed firm. Cruciform in plan, its pediment forebuilding fronts the main road. Its long, two-storey wings have a series of round-headed windows with close, goal-like glazing bars and above the centre is a white painted conical cupola.

The principal estate of the parish is *Rhug.* The Hall, in a park, was rebuilt on a new site about 1800 in blocks of light coloured Cefn stone with a high portico of four Doric columns. It is a tall, plain two-storey block with an imposing suite of ground floor rooms and, in the hall, richly carved Tudor panelling from the earlier house. On the north-east side, a wing was added about 1890 with a conservatory supported on cast iron pillars on the outside and Gothic arcades inside. The private chapel of Rhug Hall unconsecrated

and known as the Chapel of the Trinity, was built in 1637 by William Salesbury of Rhug who stoutly defended Denbigh Castle for the Royalists in the Civil Wars. Its plain rubble fabric was extensively altered in 1854 by the rebuilding of the west wall, the bellcote and all the windows. There is nothing to suggest the richness of the interior, in which late medieval and early Renaissance features expressed in a most positive form meet in a single chamber barely thirty-five feet long by twenty-five feet wide. As the public are not admitted further details are withheld by request.

The Rhug almshouses on the main Bala road are pleasant 1850 mock Jacobean, single storey with gables and stone mullioned windows. They have recently been converted into private dwellings. A.5 crosses the Dee about a mile west of the town on an impressive bridge of six spans; it carries a tablet dated 1704.

Cynwydd *see* **Llangar.**

Dinas Mawddwy *see* **Mallwyd.**

Dolgellau (5). The county town. The Wnion river, spanned by an old bridge of seven arches, contains it on its northern valley side and, to the south, the foothills rise gently to the almost vertical face of Cader Idris. Modern development on the outskirts is not unsightly and the occasional aloof 19th-century or earlier villa standing prettily in its own grounds carries the eye along the valley slope. The town itself is well contained; its architecture simple and restrained. There is contrast in the use of traditional building material, light grey granite and a rough, darker boulder stone. In later and more pretentious buildings, banks and the like, the granite is rusticated, in others smooth, in others natural. In the side streets the stones at their roughest stand out of their heavy cement rendering like currants in a bun. Decoration is rare but detail can be observed in such things as the massive stone or slate lintels of windows and doors. The layout is quite exciting, and unlike so many Welsh country towns which are of one long main street, here are small squares and blocks whose sharp edges jut

out at odd angles, casting deep shadows and causing traffic problems. Names are curiously Metropolitan, e.g. Finsbury Square, Lombard Street, Smithfield Street. The whole is predominantly early 19th century, owing much to the influence of the principal county seats in the vicinity, Nannau and Caerynwch. There are good hotels and no garish shop fronts.

The *Roman Catholic church* near the post office, was consecrated in 1967, and designed by the parish priest, Father Scalpell, a native of Malta, with professional help from the architect M. Pritchard of Blaenau Ffestiniog. The fabric is of local granite, picked from five different quarries, bluish grey in colour and shows to advantage in the massive doorway of serrated columns and interior arcades, all Norman in style. Two pillars of the south arcade are pierced by squints. The high altar and the two side altars are of stone and the whole interior restrained and free of blemish. The bronze Crucifixion hanging on the outside west wall was designed by Professor Giannino Castiglione of Milan and cast in Italy.

The *parish church of St. Mary* is early 18th century, against a plain medieval west tower. Inside, pallid but period-piece Victorian coloured glass fills all the large round-headed windows. The high boarded roof is supported on four long oak poles on either side between nave and aisles. An effigy, surprisingly unmutilated, against the north wall is of a knight from Nannau. The wall tablet nearby to Sir Richard Richards is by E. H. Baily, a pupil of Flaxman. The apse east end was added in 1864. *Harold-stone,* a private house opposite the south-west churchyard gate, is a good example of the distinctive local style.

Dr Williams' School for Girls on the Barmouth road was founded in 1875. It has a long irregular front, mainly Victorian Gothic. Two of its outlying houses, *Glyn Malden* on the Towyn road and *Dolrhyd* on the opposite side of the valley, are small 17th- and 18th-century country houses. Dolrhyd incorporates earlier dates and armorial emblems. Rows of cottages at *Pant yr Odyn* on the Towyn road, one row under

a wavy slate roof, are Victorian and very deceptive pastiches of the medieval. On rising ground opposite the northern end of the town bridge, the new Council Offices, designed in 1938 by Sir Giles Gilbert Scott on a simple effective plan of a central square block in local stone under a flat roof and two low long wings, have a fine view of the town and of Cader Idris.

The town cricket team claims to be the oldest in Wales. It was founded in 1841 by Frederick Temple, then a Balliol undergraduate, later Archbishop of Canterbury.

This recital of fact does little justice to one of the most charming country towns of Wales; intimacy is its keyword. In correspondence over the building of Brithdir church, the architect J. D. Sedding wrote of it: "What is so beautiful, seen from the hill on the station side of the river, is the sense of appropriateness, of rightness in the arrangement of slate roofs and grey and white walls. When the eye passes from the town to Cader Idris or the surrounding hills and slopes, one feels there is a sort of family likeness, a relationship between the works of man and his Maker."

Beyond the town and river, northwards, the *Torrent Walk* is open to the public, thanks to the owners of the Caerynwch estate in Brithdir parish. Either you can follow the Clwedog torrent upstream by turning down the lane about a mile out of the town on the Machynlleth road, or you can start the reverse journey at the Brithdir end. It is an entrancing walk under a variety of native trees, not at all arduous as wide shallow steps alleviate the steeper places. The scenery fulfils all the essentials of the Picturesque in drama and variety. Even in high summer the water plunges over the rocks into deep mysterious pools to which the light barely penetrates, sometimes as much as a hundred feet below the footpath; then, force spent, it glides again over its wider shallow bed. The winter force can be gauged by the uprooted trees along its banks, lying sometimes across the path of the water.

Fairbourne *see* **Llangelynin.**

Ffestiniog (1). The southern part of this famous slate parish is totally rural. A finely landscaped road winding through the Vale of Ffestiniog gives views of northern slopes banked with rhododendrons and native timber. There are two houses of interest; *Dolymoch,* now owned by the Coventry Education Committee and used throughout the year as an Outdoor Pursuit Centre for girls and boys. On

pp 108/109
DOLGELLAU

a sheltered site, seen from the Maentwrog to Ffestiniog road, it is a medium-sized house built in 1643 in two storeys of dressed stone, with dormer windows and a gabled east wing. A central, stone staircase suggests an earlier core. Two bedrooms have plaster coats of arms, each flanked by a male and female figure, and a ground floor room has a rough plaster frieze carrying coats of arms of eight ancient families of Gwynedd. Near the entrance gates, a picturesque bridge of three arches and tiny recesses spans the Goedol stream.

Outflow from Llyn Stwlan reservoir

The other house, *Plâs Tanybwlch,* is a much grander affair in a setting of romantically contrived gardens, plantations and parkland sloping to the vale. Outwardly it is a large Victorian castle, embattled on all sides, mullion windowed, entered through an arched gatehouse with sham portcullis. Along its front runs a wide terrace. It was the house of the Oakeley family, pioneers of the slate industry, who did most of the building hereabouts in long-shaped dressed slate slabs, including the wayside *Oakeley Arms Hotel* and much of *Maentwrog* village. In 1824 Lord Rothschild, granted a monopoly of mineral rights in the Welsh hills, trespassed on the Oakeley land and unsuccessfully defended an action for trespass in the High Court.

Above the Oakeley Arms Hotel a road, signposted Rhydd, leads past Llyn Mair (favoured for picnics) and Tanybwlch Station (beware of motor-coaches) into the *Coedydd Maentwrog National Nature Reserve,* bought by the National Trust and leased to the Nature Conservancy. It extends over one hundred and eighty acres, mainly of old oak woodlands, running for nearly two miles along the foothills of the Moelwyn mountains and rising to about six hundred feet above the valley floor. It has a variety of wild life, including badger, red squirrel, pied flycatcher, lesser redpoll and a number of uncommon moths. Certain footpaths and rights of way already exist in these woods. An easy approach is by a gate leading to a footpath on the right hand side of the Rhydd (Tanybwlch Station) road above the Oakeley Arms Hotel. For further information apply to the Regional Officer, Nature Conservancy, Penrhos Road, Bangor, Caerns.

Ffestiniog village has nothing of interest. The church of St Michael on a commanding site west of the village was rebuilt in 1844 and a restoration about 1910 retained the west gallery. Other features of its now lofty interior are the foil-shaped arc of the chancel arch and the glass of the three-light Victorian east window, an intricate affair of blues and reds in which a series of circles, three in each side light and four in the centre, depict incidents in the life and teaching of Christ, to illustrate such virtues as compassion, charity and forgiveness. Rather depressing cement-rendered walls. Thomas Love Peacock married the rector's daughter, Jane Griffiths, his "wild Snowdonian antelope".

Northward the character of the landscape changes to that of a mining valley of south Wales. The main road becomes a street of terrace houses, shops and chapels, seemingly interminable until at its northern

above FFESTINIOG and the Moelwyns
The Llyn Stwlan reservoir dam
is below the right peak
below BLAENAU FFESTINIOG

outlet to open country the spoil of the Oakeley and Llechwedd quarries is massed on either side. This is Blaenau Ffestiniog, on a wet day a depressing enough place, but with an industrial personality and character as strong as the countryside in which it is set. Only about three hundred men now work the slate quarries which at their peak employed some three thousand. The only alternative industrial work is at a light engineering plant making food machinery and at a clothing factory, but as yet there seems little hope for young people despite the efforts of the local authorities. Its best building is the 1914–18 Memorial Hospital, designed by Clough Williams Ellis; sited to the north-west of the town with wide views of the fierce landscape to the west, it has a small central block of two storeys with colonnaded wings on either side. St David's church, bordering the main street and built in 1842, has nothing of special interest. On the eastern boundary of the parish, the galleries of the Manod quarries, far under the mountain, which are still being worked but on a much reduced scale, housed, during the last war, pictures from London's National Gallery.

The Ffestiniog Railway was officially opened in 1836 to carry slates to the seaboard at Portmadoc; passengers were first carried in 1865. With the decline of the slate industry and road competition for passenger traffic, the line closed in 1946. Eight years later, a group of enthusiasts, despite formidable legal and financial obstacles, took the line over, to operate it as a voluntarily supported society; gradually services were extended from the Portmadoc end, reaching Tanybwlch (fourteen miles) in 1958. 320,000 passengers were carried in 1969 and preparations are in hand to complete the restoration of the last five miles to Blaenau Ffestiniog. Further information and an excellent Guide Book (3s) are available to callers at the Harbour Station at the eastern entrance to Portmadoc. (*See also* Moelwyn.)

Gwyddelwern (3). Council house development gives a rather brooding

opposite and right
BLAENAU FFESTINIOG

look to this main-road village. The church of St Beuno was much rebuilt, and a tower with an attractive but alien spire added, in 1880. But it has a fine panelled medieval roof over the sanctuary. The chancel has a good 15th-century east window with clear glass, and 17th century and earlier oak panels are mounted on the walls or incorporated in the modern chancel screen. 18th-century tablets include one to the Humphreys family of Maerdu and in the porch there are two single-light windows, one sadly damaged, with rather pallid medieval stained-glass figures. Otherwise the spacious interior is late Victorian and the green-washed, plastered walls impart melancholy. A picturesque yew tree in the churchyard has in its shade a handsome 18th-century tomb with carved emblems on the side panels and, hidden nearby in the grass, a row of low kneeling stones at the foot of graves,

each with two semi-circular openings.

On the north of the parish is considerable quarrying of the western hills and large building material works on the plain below. Here a lane to *Melin y Wig* on the Denbighshire border gives fine valley views. The old mill now uses electricity instead of water, and corn, drying on a tiled floor above a kiln, gives off a rich and heady smell. There is picturesque-in-miniature scenery along the boulder banks of the upper reaches of the river Clwyd.

Harlech *see* **Llandanwg.**

Llanaber (4). Extends north of the Mawddach estuary into the slopes of the desolate Rhinog range, whence south-flowing torrents have cleft deep valleys down to the estuary. This is the scene of the great bonanza of the mid-19th century when the *Clogau mine,* west of Cwm Mynach, yielded

fifteen thousand ounces of gold between 1844 and 1865. The speculative fever of the mid-Victorians and their readiness to take a chance turned Dolgellau into a small-scale Dawson City, and the trail was littered with abandoned machinery, prospectors' diggings and bankruptcies of the over credulous. A later, more scientific and more successful exploitation came between 1903 and 1907 and, until it closed some four years ago, the Clogau mine, one of several in the district and the traditional source of gold for Royal wedding rings, is estimated to have yielded one hundred and twenty thousand ounces. There is now talk of reopening it and of seeking the rich vein of gold thought to run from Barmouth to Bontddu.

The estuary road, one of the most beautiful in north Wales, has southward views of Cader Idris, and its hillside is dotted with charming country houses, notably *Glan y Mawddach,* whose flowering shrubs and rock and water gardens are open to the public on a specified day in early summer, under the National Gardens Scheme. *Caerdeon,* three miles or so to the east, a smaller country house, was built about 1850 for the Rev. W. E. Jelf, who retired to Wales and coached undergraduates in the classics. He built the church of St Philip, on the hillside above his house, so that he and his pupils could attend English services; much to the annoyance of the rector of Llanaber who invoked a law of Queen Elizabeth that services in predominantly Welsh areas had to be in Welsh. This led to much wrangling, and to the passing of the 1863 English Services in Wales Act which legalised English services whenever ten or more persons in a parish requested them. Jelf, aided by the Rev. J. L. Petit, modelled his church on village churches in the Basque mountains, and it suits its surroundings admirably. The fabric is of local rust coloured shale, split into horizontal slabs, under a blue grey slate roof. The outside verandah, its pent roof supported on two square pillars of narrow stone courses, is typical of Basque village churches. Above the chancel arch is an open saddleback belfry of four bells which are rung by a pulley and wheel from outside at ground level. The interior is spacious and light, with a north transept leading from the raised chancel. Stone slab floors except at the east end, single-light Kempe style stained glass in the east window; 1900 gold and mosaic reredos and four elegant, tall candleholders of spiral brass; the whole quite a showpiece. 1927 lychgate. Samuel Holland, one of the pioneers of the north Wales slate industry, died at Caerdeon in 1892 and is buried in the churchyard above the house. At the age of eighteen, his father sent him from Liverpool to Ffestiniog to superintend the working of a concession to quarry slate on the Oakeley estate. His diary recounts how he crossed the Dee estuary by boat and walked the rest of the way carrying his carpet bag. He was the chief founder of Dr Williams School for Girls, Dolgellau, and M.P. for Merioneth.

The parish church of St Mary is on the coast road north of Barmouth. A long approach is lined with white marble tombstones which show every symbol of parting and bereavement in the stone-mason's pattern book. (A notice in the porch discourages these.) From the west wall there is a wide view of the shore below and the bare caravan camps. The church interior, through an Early-English doorway of four columns, each with triple shafts—surprisingly ornate for these parts—resembles the nave of a medieval cathedral in miniature. North and south aisles divided from the nave by trans-Norman five-bay arcades supporting pointed arches. There are small pointed clerestory windows, and a graceful Early-English lancet in the east wall. An 1858 restoration was supervised by William Wynne of Peniarth and was as sympathetic as his other work at Towyn and Llanegryn.

Egryn Abbey, off the main coast road, is now a private house.

Llanbedr (4). Called the best kept village in Wales, it is helped by the bridge over the Artro and the rose-decked front of the low built *Victoria Hotel.* Besides its varied collection of shells (found on Mochras beach in Llanenddwyn parish), the hotel has well laid out gardens with a parapet above the river; in summer family parties impart quite a Sunday Continental air. Inside, for the winter, it has an inviting bar, with rounded settles at the hearth of a traditional Welsh simnai fawr (open fireplace) and gleaming brass.

The village is substantial. Tall gabled houses, stone built and tree shaded, with heavy bargeboards and finials, rise above the earlier terraced houses. St Peter's church, bellcote and much restored, is off the main road north of the bridge. Inside, its unplastered rubble walls carry many brass memorials, modern except for one on the north wall of the chancel recording burials from 1594 to 1783. A stone with incised spiral is against the inside north wall of the nave, and above the doorway a slate slab (taken from Llandanwg church) has a verse in Welsh by Matthew Owen of Llangar, saying that no one should enter this holy place and the presence of God unless he is of a good mind.

Roads branch at the bridge, west past modern villas and along the riverside to the sea at Mochras, and east inland up the *Artro valley,* a rest from the main road. About a mile up the valley the road branches to Cwm Bychan and Cwm Nantcol. both gateways to the Rhinogs (*q.v.*) Near where they part, Salem Baptist chapel is worth seeing for its domestic 18th-century architecture. The interior provided the setting, and its members the models, for a painting by Sydney Curnow Vosper, shown at the 1909 Royal Academy, and now in the Lever Gallery, Port Sunlight. The erect figure of a tight-lipped old lady, in traditional Welsh dress and holding a prayer book, dominates it. Reproductions, chosen for the picture's nostalgic evocation of the past, are in thousands of Welsh homes and in many lands (see page 73).

Llandanwg (4). *Harlech* dominates this small coastal parish with its fortress, rising from the rocks above the plain from which the sea has receded; so much so that its water-gate is nearly a mile inland. Though tamed by the Ministry of Public Building and Works, it is still a formidable reminder of alien conquest. Built by Edward I about 1290 as part of his coastal chain of castles, it has survived the "drums and tramplings" of many conquests. It surrendered to Owain Glyndwr in 1404 to be recaptured by the English four years later, was besieged and surrendered to the Yorkists in the Wars of the Roses. It decayed after the accession of the Tudor line, until, again besieged in the Civil Wars, it surrendered in 1647, the last Royalist stronghold in Britain. Its outstanding feature, unique in the great Edwardian castles of north Wales, is the gatehouse on the landward side. At each corner of the curtain walls, which contain the four-sided inner ward, circular towers defend its flanks and partly explain why the castle has only once been taken by storm.

Landward of the castle, a town developed, with steep access from the plain, but more easily entered by the upper coastal road. It is a place of narrow, twisting streets, its architecture covering many styles and periods. *Plâs,* early 18th-century, now a cafe, is distinguished by its closely-sashed square windows. The church of St Tanwg, built in the 1840s as a single chamber with a west gallery, has been modified; today it has a light airy interior with clear glass in Gothic windows, and white walls. Chairs, and stained glass by Celtic Studios in a south window. A tall 15th-century font from the old church is richly carved and unusually elegant. Granite built, substantial houses among a profusion of flowering shrubs stand back on the hillside from the upper coastal road, enjoying wide western views.

Harlech attracts golfers to the famous championship-class *Royal St Davids Golf Course* (Royal from the patronage of the Duke of Windsor), laid out below the Royal St Davids Hotel on the flat sandy plain, fringed by dunes. *Coleg Harlech,* residential and for adult education, is a granite building of 1910 in the traditional Merioneth style of the 1830s. Stretches of yellow shore.

North of Harlech, seen across meadows from the Talsarnau road, *Lasynys* is a small Elizabethan house built into a rocky knoll on the plain, in such a way that it is partly three- and partly two-storeyed with a small courtyard contrived on the upper level in a 1715 alteration. It was the home of the Rev. Ellis Wynne (d. 1734), rector of Llandanwg and author of *Y Bardd Cwsg* (*The Poet asleep*). From this remote, untroubled place he thundered against the vices of the age.

The old church of St Tanwg, abandoned now except for an occasional summer service, lies at the southern tip of the parish on the sea-shore. Approached from the main coast road down a narrow lane sign-posted Llandanwg Beach with close-up views of dry stone walls and barns, it lies desolate, windows and door shuttered against the rising drifts of blown sand, in which flat slate tombstones bear dates from the early 18th century. Traditionally a chapel of rest for corpses carried to the holy burial ground of Bardsey Island, it is a simple single chamber with an early 15th-century east window under an exterior pointed hood. Enquire for further information at the obliging, something-for-every-body, shop in the nearby car park.

Llandderfel (3). Best approached from the Bala to Llandrillo road which crosses the Dee on an old bridge of four arches low over the water. To the south is the park of *Pale* (accent on the *e*) *Hall,* built of light cinnamon-coloured Cefn stone in the baronial style in 1870, probably by S. Pountney Smith of Shrewsbury, for Henry Robertson. Later it became part of the Westminster estates and is now empty. Henry Robertson (1816–1878), M.P. for Shrewsbury and later Merioneth, designed and engineered a network of railways radiating from Shrewsbury, as well as the railway from Ruabon to Bala and viaducts over the Dee and Ceiriog. He was an original partner in Beyer, Peacock & Co., locomotive builders. His railway connections are preserved in a carved stone on the portico of Pale Hall showing the forepart of a Rocket type engine and the motto *Ex Fumo Dare Lucem.*

The best house in the parish is *Crogen,* in a park off the Llandrillo road east of the bridge. With roots far back in Welsh history, it is a small, beautifully-composed country house with an 1800-ish Gothic front and, on an upper floor, the top of a 14th-century window.

To the west along the Dee valley is the estate of *Bodweni Hall,* an irregular stone-built house dating from 1561, with a strong Puritan tradition and one of the first licensed preaching houses in the county. It has been much modernised.

The appearance of the hillside village which slopes into a lovely valley is marred at its northern approach by the back view of early council house development. The church of St Derfel, in the centre of the village, was restored in the 1870s by S. Pountney Smith. It has an east window with 16th-century tracery and a carved screen of the same period. Otherwise the interior, within white plastered walls, is Victorian, well cared for. A stuffed white owl under a glass dome on a window-ledge is for scaring away bats. In the porch is a wooden figure of a horse and by its side a ringed staff of painted wood. The horse once carried a rider, reputedly the Celtic Saint Derfel Gadern, and had magic properties, one of them being the power to put out forest fires. It was removed to London in 1535 when Thomas Cromwell's commissioners purged churches of their idolatries, and with a touch of the macabre it formed part of the execution pyre of the Greenwich friar Father Forest. Ford Madox Ford recreated the scene in his book *The Fifth Queen.* The statue is represented as red-cheeked, coat and limbs painted green, wearing a gilt helmet, carrying a great spear and towering as high as the gallows.

The road north from the village to *Bethel* on the main Corwen to Bala road is narrow but pretty. On this main road an outlying 1864 church at *Glan yr Afon* was designed by Sir Gilbert Scott. A Welsh inscription below a rich Victorian stained glass east window states that it was built in memory of Robert and Frances Uchan (or Vaughan) of Rhug and Nannau by their friends and neighbours. The interior, although small, gives an impression of space and freedom; the tiled chancel floor and lower part of the east wall are very handsome. West of this hamlet the main road climbs out of the Dee valley, and the hills close in on it, steeply wooded on the south side, and small farmsteads are dotted in the green pasture below the high bracken on the north; then the valley opens again in marshy land at *Sarnau.*

In the south of the parish, a narrow enclave between Aberhirnant Forest and the Ceiriog valley takes in the steep road into the Berwyns from the Dee valley near Pale Hall to *Milltir Cerrig* and thence downhill to Llangynog in Montgomeryshire. Moorland and forestry plantations and views of deep valleys.

Llandrillo (3). Quite a substantial village of low 18th-century stone-built, white and grey washed houses; one such, opposite the church gates, is dated 1748. The *Dudley Arms Hotel* has a pleasant 19th-century front. The church of St Trillo was rebuilt in 1877 (architect S. Pountney Smith, Shrewsbury). The fabric incorporates bits and pieces of the earlier building. The interior is high,

Dovecote at Tyfos,
LLANDDERFEL

draughty and rather gloomy with grey plastered walls, some rich Victorian glass in the chancel and 1936 painted glass by Geoffrey Webb on the north wall of the nave; this in three lights, and to the memory of John Evans, depicts the crossing from Brittany to Wales of Saints Cadfan and Ithel Hael and their missionary work with St Trillo, son of Ithel Hael. A plain octagonal 15th-century font is in the vestry and an 18th-century communion table; otherwise all furnishing is Victorian. Against the outside south wall a canopied Wynne tomb of 1706 was sadly misused, at the time of our visit, as a dumping place for old slates and sandbags. Good hillside views from the churchyard. The tall pink and grey-fronted gabled chapel (1870-ish, but no inscriptions) on the Bala road is an eyecatcher.

A narrow road south from the village climbs out of the Ceiriog valley at Pennant to end in the yard of *Blaencwm*, a substantial farmhouse, stone built and dated 1728. Immediately beyond, the forest clad slopes of the Berwyn range rise steeply. In the north of the parish, where there are cairns and barrows, remote *Llyn Mynyllod* has a floating island, said to move towards Corwen or Bala as market prices rise at either town.

A tall avenue of beech and chestnut trees, shading a stream and masking an unobtrusive caravan park, leads from an ancient barn on the main road to Corwen to the early 19th-century farmhouse of *Hendwr*. The house with its pretty lattice windows was rebuilt about 1830 to replace a 1660 building and from its design, especially the tall porch, it probably followed the plan of the original house.

Llanddwywe is y Graig (4). A narrow parish bisected by the river *Ysgethin* which rising in Lake Bodlyn below the precipices of Dyffwys mountain, nears the end of its short journey at the pretty, tree-shaded village of *Talybont,* on the coast road from Barmouth to Harlech. Its exposed sea-front is a chain of caravan and holiday camps. Its church (dedication obscure, probably to St Ddywai) is at the northern end of Talybont, a simple single chamber

with a rather savagely repointed exterior. The porch is dated 1593 and the three light east window is probably contemporary with it. The restored interior is pleasant with green tinted walls under a good 16th-century roof. A feature is the 1615 Cors y Gedol chapel of the Vaughan family, forming the north transept and entered through an openwork oak screen. Its stone memorials include an elaborate early 17th-century group of kneeling parents and children (one baby in arms), and a tomb for William Vaughan, late 18th-century, by Vander Hagen of Shrewsbury.

Cors y Gedol one of the main houses of the county lies up a long drive leading from the main road opposite the church. It has gradually evolved from the east wing built in 1576, though alterations in 1660 which added a west wing, reconstructed and decorated in Adam style in 1782, until the 19th century, when new rooms on the north side more than doubled the size of the house. On the ground floor of the east block a heavily panelled room under a particularly fine beamed ceiling has a stone-arched fireplace dated 1594 and the inscription, *Sequere justitiam et invenias vitam.* Upper rooms are similarly panelled. There is an imposing, free-standing gatehouse built in 1630 and attributed locally to Inigo Jones, possibly adapted from one of his designs. A large stone barn dated 1685 lies to the south east of the house and there are other subsidiary buildings, including a farmhouse, now the main dwelling. A house of consequence but, although furnished and maintained, little used. Visitors are not encouraged.

Llanddwywe uwch y Graig (4). *Upper Llanddwywe,* a bare, almost uninhabited parish of mountain and moorland, has no common boundary with its coastal namesake. Its eastern boundary is the woodland of Coed y Brenin on the west side of the Dolgellau to Ffestiniog road. Apart from a few houses on this road there seems nothing to justify its status as a parish. See Llanelltud for Rhaiadr Du waterfall.

Llandecwyn (1). High and lonely on a hill above Talsarnau stands the 1879 church of St Tecwyn, with a bellcote,

locked and seemingly friendless. Round it is a fierce uninhabited landscape of ridges and lonely lakes. The main road south of the Dwyryd estuary is the northern boundary.

Llanegryn (7). A long narrow parish stretching from the Dysynni valley over the mountains along the old road almost to the Mawddach estuary. The only populated part is the south. The rest is grazing. The village lies compactly in a hollow off the coastal Towyn to Dolgellau road. Cottages and shops line a short street leading down to a stream, across which stand two chapels joined into one block by their vestries; *Bethel* (1867) with round-headed windows on either side of a central door, and *Ebenezer* (1816–1922), more elaborate with double doors, three round-headed windows and an obelisk to Hugh Owen (1637–1699) whom an inscription in Welsh proclaims to have been one of the first ministers of the Independent (Congregational) movement in north Wales.

The bellcoted church of St Mary and St Egryn lies on high ground about half a mile north-west of the village. Approached through a lych gate with a pretty barge board, down a path lined with slate, silver-inscribed tombstones, it has a weathered exterior of rubble and large dressed stones, and a porch with slate seats. Fairly extensively restored in 1878, but two 13th-century windows remain in the south wall. Its glory, and one of the glories of medieval woodwork, is the 15th-century rood loft and screen, supposed to have come from Cymmer Abbey in Llanelltud parish. The pierced work of the screen is elaborate and delicate and the frames and panels are carved in abstract and random designs, sometimes including spirals and strapwork, Celtic in tradition and inspiration. Its remoteness probably saved it. Against it, the rest of the interior might well seem insignificant; the nave certainly does, but the sanctuary glows with a good late Victorian stained glass window by H. Hughes, London, three lights, flanked by two elaborate memorials to Peniarth families. The medieval font has a scalloped underside on a circular pillar. Paraffin lamps, clear glass lattice windows on white walls,

LLANEGRYN: The rood loft

a tiny organ with unpainted pipes by Ginn Bros, Merton, and a good 20th-century tablet on the north wall of the nave to Owen Slaney Wynne of Peniarth.

Peniarth, one of the principal houses of the county is sited on the flat valley floor. The long straight drive to it and the clump of trees hiding it give it an air of the Low Countries, dispelled on closer acquaintance by the natural layout of the ground and the soft native green of the park. The house, very large by Welsh standards, bears an air of architectural informality. Largely rebuilt of local rubble in 1700 on original 15th-century or earlier foundations, its front elevation was then refaced in locally fired bricks, now beautifully mellowed (this is the only use of brick in any building of con-sequence in the western part of the county). At the same time a free standing building of similar brick was built in 1727 near and at right angles to the main block, to be capped in 1812 by a bell tower. The front elevation of the main block was carried forward at ground level in the 19th century in brick to enlarge the entrance hall. This gives an impressive interior view of Georgian domestic elegance.

Peniarth has never passed out of the hands of some branch of its original owners, of whom, within recent history W. W. E. Wynne of Peniarth (1801–1880) is best known. An amateur architect, he supervised the restoration of Llanaber, Towyn, and Llanegryn churches, wherein he showed excellent discretion. He owned an incomparable collection of manuscripts of Welsh history, part of which came from Hengwrt, Llanelltud. They are now in the National Library of Wales, Aberystwyth

Llanelltud (4). A small parish, running north from the upper Mawddach estuary and flanked on the east by the Ganllwyd valley. On the river bank at the head of the estuary *Cymmer Abbey* was founded at the end of the 12th century by a colony of Cisterian monks from Cymhir in Radnorshire, and was their smallest Welsh monastery. Three lofty Early English lancet windows at the east end and three smaller ones in the south wall are left standing. The serenity which lingers in such places is disturbed by adjacent caravans but there is a Cotmanesque feeling about the scene on the farm-house side. In the small, trim wayside village the church of St Illtyd is on rising ground; a simple building with pretty round-headed 19th-century windows, foundation of rough boulders, setting of yews and slate tomb stones which all give it character. Inside, a hatchment of the Vaughan family of Hengwrt hangs on the west wall. A photograph shows a silver gilt chalice and paten found on a neighbouring hillside, by two gold prospectors, now in the National Museum, Cardiff. They probably came from Cymmer Abbey, and originated in Westphalia. *Hengwrt* was recently destroyed by fire; a watercolour by the painter of Welsh houses, Moses Griffiths, shows it as an early Georgian block with a deep parapet and well spaced windows. Robert Vaughan (1592–1667) of Hengwrt, antiquary and bibliophile, had a collection of manuscripts and books that are now in the National Library, Aberystwyth.

The village is the starting or finishing point for one of two Precipice Walks, well named, each taking about three hours and with far and close views of forest, estuary and mountains. The other, the New Precipice Walk can start near Cymmer Abbey and finish beyond Dolgellau.

Up the Ganllwyd valley, 1833 *Tyn y Groes Hotel* is a pretty stone building of two storeys with black and white gables over square-framed windows. On the other side of the road there is a sheer drop to the

119

Mawddach river. In the 19th-century gold rush hereabouts this was a favourite resort of miners, speculators and prospectors. Up the valley, *Dolmelynllyn Hall* on National Trust land, is a tall Victorian building now an hotel and, nearby, up against a corrugated iron chapel a gateway off the main road leads to *Rhaiadr Du waterfall,* formed by the Camlan stream; an ideal place for a picnic under the oaks and among the boulders, softly padded with moss.

Llanenddwyn (4). The wild untracked inland area of this parish is dotted with Bronze and Iron Age cairns, hill forts and hut circles. The Neolithic Age has left two dolmens at the back of the village school at the southern entrance to the village of *Dyffryn Ardudwy,* the main settlement. Spaced close together they are not very impressive, and the capstone of one is the shape of a tortoise shell.

The older village is around the church of St Enddwyn, a female Celtic saint, seaward from the main road. The church was largely rebuilt in 1883 using older materials in the fabric. It has an open 16th-century roof, two short transepts and benefaction boards in the porch. Old material includes a finial dated 1588 and a spiral incised stone in the gable of the lychgate.

From the next village of Llanbedr a road runs due west past an aerodrome to the peninsular of *Mochras* or *Shell Island*; it can be reached by car over a causeway one and a half hours before and after high tide. A charge (currently 5s per car) is made for access through the farm, worth it for the views of the northern and eastern mountains. There are also stretches of sand, rocky pools at low tide, dunes and a variety of shells (*see* Llanbedr). An outbuilding of Mochras Farm has a fine example in its gable end of a dry stone wall, in which some of the lower stones are more than a yard long. The early 17th-century farm house, modernised inside, is impervious to the western gales. Its loneliness is broken by low-flying planes and, in the summer, by many visitors (*see also* Introduction).

Llanfachreth (5). Its southern boundary runs west above the Wnion valley

for about six miles from the outskirts of Dolgellau along the Roman road to Bala. At *Rhydymain,* off the main road, there is a 1962 brick-built village hall, some neat terrace cottages and a sad gabled chapel, whose large graveyard is bordered by tall Irish yews. Nearby, *Hengwrt,* now an hotel, is a massive 1892 stone-built house (Tudor style, with long oriel windows) with fine views. It replaced a 1790 house destroyed by fire in 1885. The staircase was made and carved in India. But the main interest of the parish lies in the north; in the tangle of lanes, steep and twisting, lined with scrub oak and boulders, with an occasional view of hanger woods across the valley to the south, and always in winter the noise of tumbling water; in the small stone-walled enclosures, abandoned as pasture and now clothed with plantations. Also in an eyecatcher gateway, some fifteen feet high at the *Garreg Fawr* pillar box, the sides built of rubble courses and the capstone a huge boulder brought from Harlech. According to local report this was built to give employment after the Napoleonic wars by Sir Robert Vaughan, squire of Nannau. The village clings picturesquely to the hillside. The church of St Machreth was rebuilt in 1874 (architect E. B. Ferrey), the old tower having been recapped with a spire about one hundred years earlier. It is steeply approached up cobbled steps through the south lychgate, built, as elegant slate slabs on its north facing side testify in English and Welsh, to the memory of George III "to promote the religion which he loved and practised". The church inside is Victorian, except for wall tablets. Stained glass of 1887 in the three-light east window is by Ward and Hughes. The principal tablet, on the west wall, is a massive swagged and draped memorial stone with the head and shoulders in relief of Anne Nanney of Nanney Hall "wife of Hugh Nanney, M.P. Colonel of Militia and Vice Admiral of N. Wales in the reign of William the Third, died 1739". Other memorials, two by S. & F. Franceys, Liverpool, and T. Gaffin, London, are mainly to members of the Vaughan family of Nannau; the best, unsigned, to Rice Jones, poet, of Blaenau, is early 19th

century, with a female figure. Priests' chairs in the sanctuary are heavy Jacobean. Alabaster altar and reredos. Between the church and the good-looking 19th-century village school and schoolhouse there is a pretty row of gabled cottages, whose slate roof verandah is supported on pillars of alternate square stones and rounded bricks.

The Vaughan family owned much of the land in these parts. Their pretty cottages and farmhouses, square, stonebuilt and often with tall chimneys, adorn the landscape. *Nannau,* seen from the Llanfachreth to Dolgellau road across the park is a three-storeyed, granite built Georgian house (1796) with a parapet, central balustrade and two low wings. It is at least the fifth house to be known as Nannau, one having been burnt by Owain Glyndwr in 1404. It passed out of the Vaughan family in 1964. One of the Nannau treasures is a bucket of sheet bronze; found in a peat bog in nearby Arthog where it had been left about 700 B.C., perhaps as a votive offering, it originated in the Danube Valley and is of a type unknown otherwise in Britain, marking the progress of the late Bronze Age settlers from Europe.

A single-track lane, narrow, and steep in parts leads north from the village into the forest of *Coed y Brenin* and through it in Swiss-like environment of forest and cascade, into the Eden valley at Ganllwyd.

Pistyll y Cain might have been designed by some brilliant landscape gardener. It is the most Japanese-looking of all waterfalls in the British Isles. Its fall is steep on the side of the viewer in a delicate series of descending stairs that cause the water to splash from each step to the one below it. The neighbouring *Rhaiadr Mawddach,* painted by Samuel Palmer on his Welsh tour (one of his rare oil paintings, from drawings made on the spot, it is now in the Tate Gallery) is more sudden and impetuous. Both are hidden in high woods of birch and sessile oaks and rowan, with little Japanese-style rocky eminences rising above the trees in truly Romantic manner. Ruined workings for gold (mined and washed here since Roman times until 1939) neighbour them northward at Gwynfynydd. One approach is by the

Cymmer Abbey, LLANELLTUD

lane from Ganllwyd, along the public road through Coed y Brenin forest keeping the river Mawddach always on your right. The Youth Hostel marked on the Ordnance Survey maps appears disused but you pass a short terrace of houses probably connected with the gold mines, and the burnt out shell of a larger house, perhaps where the mine's captain lived. The road is then barred by a gate marked private but it is a short ten minute walk to the falls. An option recently taken on the base mineral rights of about seven hundred acres near Dol-gellau includes the Gwynfynydd gold mine, and covers exploration for gold,

silver, lead, zinc and copper, using methods unknown when such mines were closed.

Llanfair (4). Sea views from the coast road. The small church of St Mary lies on the main road up a path bordered by Irish yews, and the churchyard is thick with slate tomb-stones. Victorian furniture, white walls, lancet windows with clear glass and a fine, well preserved 15th-century roof. The oak chancel screen of heavy balusters above a panelled lower half is late 16th or early 17th century. Long narrow nave, raised

chancel and sanctuary and the whole combining to form a beautiful, well loved interior. The north wall has well lettered slate tablets in wooden frames to the Owen family of Crafnant naming their forebears back to the 16th century.

Crafnant, now a simple farmhouse with some dry stone walling in its outbuildings, is alongside the narrow but entrancing road which follows the Artro stream, the parish bound-ary, along the upper reaches of Cwm Bychan. It is a car-frequented road in summer and should be treated with caution, especially as it nears Cwm Bychan.

Llanfihangel y Pennant (7) The south-western slopes of Cader Idris close in the narrowing Dysynni valley on three sides, and the road peters out on the valley floor where tall beech trees form an avenue to a farmhouse and a stream is broken by boulders into many rivulets. The ruins of Mary Jones' cottage stand here; a memorial records that "in the year 1800 at the age of eighteen she walked from here to Bala to procure from the Rev. Thomas Charles, B.A. a copy of the Welsh Bible. This incident was the occasion of the formation of the British and Foreign Bible Society". Tradition says she walked barefooted. Down the valley, where the pasture is as level and green as a billiard table and dotted with Welsh Black cattle, is the village: no more than a few cottages round the church of St Michael, which is set in a circular churchyard. Small 18th-century sundial, and many well-cut slate tombstones. Inside, a plain open chamber, bare of ornament, with clear glass except at the east end, cream walls, hanging paraffin lamps and low box pews; scalloped medieval font. In the north wall a door opens on to a large transept, stone flagged, empty and primitive under its open roof of rough untreated timber. It has a crude 15th-century window of two openings.

Castell y Bere, a Welsh fortress, was built by Llywelyn the Great about 1221, and taken by the English in 1283, on a rocky knoll rising from the valley bed. Its outlines and layout which follow the contours of the grey, quartz-veined rock have recently been exposed from a tangle of undergrowth by the Ministry of Public Building and Works, and a close look at it is well worth the short walk. It calls to mind a picture of a Crusader fort with scrub oak on the rising ground reproducing the shapes of olive trees. Places of such haunting beauty are rare. From the low ramparts there is a view down the valley which would have delighted the 18th-century romantic artist; the mountains are on either side and, on the southern flank, the bold, towering outline of *Craigyr Aderyn*, or *Birds Rock*, in Llanegryn parish.

Caer Berllan on the road out of the valley to Talyllyn is a perfect, small

17th-century manor house. If the stone were lighter coloured it could be in the Cotswolds. Low-walled raised terrace garden in front, and pillared entrance. The road over the pass into the Talyllyn valley has views, following the mountainside above the slate miners' village of *Abergynolwyn*.

Llanfor (2). A large parish, astride the middle of the county from its northern to southern boundaries. Its centre, comprising the church of St Deinol, rectory, smithy and a few cottages is on the main road, a mile or so east of Bala. The church was rebuilt and its old tower recapped with a saddle back roof in 1874 (architect, E. B. Ferrey). Its high, rather gaunt interior is Victorian, and Munich-type glass adds to the darkness of the chancel. There is 20th-century stained glass by Seward and Co. A Union Jack and the colours of the Merionethshire Militia (deposited in June 1914) hang from the rafters. Price family of Rhiwlas hatchment on west wall, and Price and Bulkeley 18th-century tablets inside the porch. Medieval panels in the modern chancel screen. In the churchyard is the Price mausoleum, built after Bendigo won the Kempton Park Jubilee in 1887. The inscription over the doorway is much quoted:

> "As to my latter end I go
> to win my Jubilee
> I thank my good horse Bendigo
> who built this tomb for me."

A lane heads north from the village to pretty little *Pantglas* chapel, 1903, hardly large enough to overtop the boulders which hem it in. *Rhiwlas* on the hillside above the junction of the Dee and Treweryn rivers was demolished in 1955 and a smaller house built on the site from old materials and in the traditional style of the early 19th century (architect, Clough Williams Ellis). Fine old outbuildings with castle-type 1800-ish gateway remain. The house has a fine view of Bala and Treweryn gorge.

The northern half of the parish extends into the Snowdonia National Park; there is a small settlement of *Fron Goch* and a small wayside church, built in 1857. R. J. Lloyd Price of Rhiwlas started a whisky distillery here in 1887, drawing water

from the Tairvelyn brook. A pamphlet described the product as "the most wonderful whisky that ever drove the skeleton from the feast or painted landscapes in the brain of man". Queen Victoria and the Prince of Wales accepted samples, but the enterprise was shortlived. Augustus John was a strong advocate of its revival. After the Irish rising in 1916 the buildings were used as an internment camp; then they were demolished, and there must have been much searching of teetotal conscience before some of the material was used for rebuilding the Methodist chapel and vestry at Talybont.

The southern half of the parish is forest and mountain—barely penetrable except through the Hirnant valley from *Rhos y Gwaliau*, by the mountain road to Lake Vyrnwy through forest and high moorland, an exciting, and in some places cliff-hanging, road. At Rhos y Gwaliau, in a picturesque setting of streams and boulders, a footbridge leads to the small, lofty and entirely Victorian church of the Holy Trinity (1880 by E. B. Ferrey). An inscription in the churchyard records that Henry Richardson of Aberhirnant the inventor of the Tubular Lifeboat, caused the church to be built. Richardson was an army officer and his invention, named the *Challenger*, was launched in 1852. Her maiden voyage from New Brighton on the Wirral to Ramsgate took two hundred and thirteen hours at sea. Near the church *Plâs Rhiw-Waedog*, now a youth hostel, is a Jacobean once quadrangular manor house (1664) of the Lloyd family with a very early history. It has elaborate 17th-century fireplaces, an oak staircase and big cellars. There are legends about underground passages. The gatehouse has been modernised. An adjacent farm has a splendid enclosure of outbuildings. The manor house site is traditionally the home of Llywarch Hên a 6th-century prince and subject of a poetry saga of the 9th century. In this Llywarch Hên sends the last of his twenty-four sons Gwen to battle and then laments having driven them all including Gwen to death because his honour lay in their display of bravery. He finally laments his loneliness and the decline of his natural powers.

123

Llanfrothen (1). From Penrhyndeu-draeth the road to Beddgelert falls steeply on to the peat marsh of *Morfa Gwyllt*. There are views of the northern mountain range and in the foothills to the north-east a sham castle built on the Brondanw estate in the 1920s gives scale and a prophetic touch of the Picturesque. Then it goes on to the small village where modern bungalows are pleasantly grouped behind the modern simple church of St Catherine. The First World War Memorial is a large cairn topped by a torch with slate memorial tablets with well-cut letters and emblems. Beyond, a short low terrace of colour-washed cottages ends with the *Brondanw Arms Inn,* a pleasant building with an elaborate wrought-iron bracket holding a gilded emblem. Beyond again are the entrance gates to Plâs Brondanw and a terrace of stone-faced cottages. *Plâs Brondanw* is the home of the Williams Ellis family which has a long tradition of land improvement and reclamation (*see also* Penrhyndeudraeth). The outline of the house can be seen from the lane leading to the mountain village of Croesor at the head of Cwm Croesor. It was rebuilt in the 1950s after a disastrous fire. *Croesor* is a small isolated settlement dominated by a large chapel at its northern end and sheltered under the ridge of Cnicht. The track to the Old Quarry is now barred to cars on the outskirts of the village; but there is a hair-raising mountain road narrow but quite suitable for cars, back to the main road near Tanybwlch Station, through the Forestry Commission's *Coed Llyn y Garnedd*. This has splendid distant views, and also close-up ones of the Moelwyn range.

Off the marsh road to Tremadoc is *Ynysfor,* in a park bounded by rhododendrons and on rising ground. It has a kennel of fox hounds maintained by the family for many generations. The pack is hunted on foot over rocky mountain country, mainly in Caernarvonshire.

The parish church of St Brothen lies behind Llan Farm, off the road to Rhyd. It is on a lonely overgrown site and noted for the occasion of David Lloyd George's first brush, as a rising solicitor in Criccieth, with the Established Church, when he enforced through the courts the right

of Nonconformist burial in parish churchyards. The church is picturesquely primitive, a simple bellcote building, in sad decay. Lancet windows at the east end indicate the 13th century; other square-headed windows are 17th or early 18th century. The original oak chancel screen has fluted shafts, rough classical detail, and oblong holes cut like water scuppers in the lower panels. A beam about seven feet long carved in a vine-leaf pattern with a finial at each end is mounted above the altar; it is known as *Y Credyn* (The Creed). Ancient chest hollowed from an oak tree trunk. The plain low box pews date from 1844, but others in the chancel and elsewhere incorporate earlier material. Clear glass in diamond paned windows, cement rendered walls, and no apparent means of artificial lighting.

Llangar (3). Most of the parish, rising nineteen hundred feet on its eastern boundary, lies on the bare northern slopes of the Berwyn range and is deeply pierced by the *Trystion valley*. On the valley's north flank a perfectly adequate road and track leads through forestry plantations and natural woodland to the edge of the moor on the county boundary whence a footpath leads down into the Ceiriog valley. Game is strictly preserved here; it is inadvisable to leave cars unattended or to stray from the rights of way. The Trystion waterfalls are within a quarter of a mile of Cynwyd's village square. Approached through a joint gate and style they rise above the ruins of a mill, *Felin Ucha*. The main stream drops through a narrow cleft into a deep pool, shaded by oaks and edged by boulders. *Cynwyd* is the only centre of population, a crossroads village of pleasant, unpretentious architecture with two seemly inns facing each other; the modern council house development looks unrelated, as if it still has to be accepted as part of the village pattern. The church of St John the Evangelist is a nave and chancel building (1856, by M. Rhode Hawkins); its simple interior suffers from painted scroll-work on the chancel arch, and gold and chocolate colour on the rafters and space between. Early 18th-century tablets (removed

from Llangar old church) to Gwerclas families include a pretty one, dated 1710.

West of the village a well-proportioned bridge of four spans with cutwaters carries traffic into a maze of lanes and rising ground. Among the lanes, *Gwerclas* is a tall mid-18th-century country house of red brick on stone foundations. It has Venetian windows on the protruding wings of the front elevation and, over the main entrance, painted arms of the Hughes and Lloyd families dated 1767. At the back, casement windows overlook a brick-walled garden and summer house, now overgrown. A wide mid-18th-century oak staircase with elegant balustrades leads to the attics of the central block. The only chapel of interest, Methodist Salem, is nearby, on higher ground at *Penrhos;* a primitive 18th-century single chamber, part of a cottage group, its original box pews seat about thirty.

Llangar old church of All Saints, abandoned except for occasional worship, is being saved at the eleventh hour from collapse by the Ministry of Public Building and Works. The fabric is medieval; box pews, three-decker pulpit, altar rails and gallery, all 17th and 18th century. Wall paintings, including the Royal Arms and Welsh inscriptions of the Lord's Prayer (probably Elizabethan) barely show through the yellow distemper, and the removal of an 18th-century plaster ceiling has revealed a medieval oak rafter roof. A 12th-century font is recessed in the south wall, and a badly torn hatchment hangs above the gallery stairs. Outside, near the south wall, in the sheep-cropped, sloping churchyard, are early 17th-century Latin inscribed tombstones of Gwerclas families. The church is above the shingle flats where the river Alwen joins the Dee. It is difficult of access, across a field from a small farmyard and along a sunken lane through an old lychgate. The sunken lane brings to mind a processional route to a thicket shrine of the Druids; indeed the whole place suggests that the origins of this site for worship are rooted in earlier beliefs and pagan mysteries. The not uncommon legend of the Devil pulling down by night what had been built by day is associated with the church, and it has been suggested that this legend has its basis in the folklore concerning the struggle between Christians and pagans for the possession of holy places.

During restoration the church has been entirely encased in corrugated sheets, clearly visible from the main road from Cynwyd to Corwen, and cannot be entered.

Llangelynin (7). The coast road north to Towyn enters the parish on high downland east of the bare hamlet of *Rhoslefain*; here opposite the wayside church of St Mary (single chamber early-Victorian with pointed lattice windows) a road branches to *Tonfanau*. At sea level, the green landscape is darkened by barracks and hutments, treeless except around sweetly named *Llanbendigaid,* an old, dormered country house. South of Tonfanau granite quarries bite into the hillside, overlooking *Broad Water*, almost a landlocked lake formed by the seaward struggles of the Dysynni.

A feature of the countryside is the dry stone walling, at its best around Tonfanau and seen to advantage on the slopes above and below the coast road. The church of St Celynin, abandoned except for the occasional summer service but still in good repair, lies on a natural cliff terrace below the main road. Outside, little more than a barn, its single chamber is medieval and primitive under a fine 15th-century roof with massive tie beams, king and queen posts and long wall brackets. The plain fabric is 12th to 13th century. On the stone flags plain early 19th-century benches, the only furniture except for the pulpit, retain original inscriptions of the names, titles and addresses of their holders. Two 1845 bronze chandeliers hang from the roof. Frescoes show faintly through the plaster of the north wall and, near them, a horse-drawn bier with shafts fore and aft, which used to carry coffins down the steep slopes. The screen was constructed partly from older material in a light 1823 restoration. Abram Wood, 18th-century founder of the Wood family of Welsh gypsies, is buried in the churchyard. His initials are visible on a prostrate, rough slate opposite the porch.

The main settlement is *Llwyngwril,* a compact village alongside the main road. The church of St Celynin was built in 1843, architect Thomas Jones of Chester, in local stone with a red sandstone belfry. The interior retains its west gallery and has been otherwise entirely refurnished. Good, rich colour in the late Victorian three-light east window. *Llwyndu,* on the eastern outskirts of the village, a simple stone-built farmhouse is associated with the Quakers. From it the Humphrey family led a band of Friends to settle in Pennsylvania early in the 18th century. Their burial ground, now used by the Methodists, lies in a small dry-walled enclosure on the opposite side of the main road; its entrance gate carries an iron plaque dated 1646.

Beyond Llwyngwril the foothills of Cader Idris rise sheer from the sea and below the main road the railway track is laid along a rock shelf. At *Friog Rocks* there have been two train disasters caused by landslides and around the rocky shoulder the road and railway drop to sea level at Fairbourne. There can be few stretches of track in Britain more exposed to the Atlantic gales.

There is a Hayling Island look about *Fairbourne* behind its coastal barrier of concrete defences against invasion. Fine golden sands but otherwise not a very pretty sight. A fifteen-inch gauge, privately-operated railway, petrol-engined and over fifty years old, carries summer passengers to and from the ferry to Barmouth. The church of St Cynon, built in 1926 into the hillside, overlooks the shore. Designed by J. B. Mendham it has gabled aisles, stained glass in the east window by William Morris, Westminster, and another smaller window by Jones and Willis. Gallery loft at west end. The pleasant, light interior is marred by rather garish walls of unplastered rubble.

The parish extends further along the estuary, to end beyond the village of Arthog at a large disused quarry of fantastic planes and levels. *Arthog* has a very pleasant row of twelve stone-built dormered cottages, *c.* 1870. Another row, the *Crescent,* also picturesque but less traditional, is hidden beyond Barmouth Junction station behind Fegla Fawr farm. In curious contrast with its wild, broken setting of rocky hillocks and scrub oaks, it is an esplanade terrace of eight three-storeyed houses faced with red brick, built about 1907 by a Cardiff patron of the arts, Solomon Andrews. It is seen to advantage from the other side of the estuary, and, as the home of artists and novelists, retains its connection with the arts. The fourth church of the parish, St Catherine's, a single-chamber building in the classical style of the 1830s, lies on the main road. Above, the hillside gardens of the principal house of the village, *Tyn y Coed,* are open to the public (enquire at the Estate Shop on the main road). The house, built in 1878 and said locally to have been designed by Pugin, is of grey granite with lighter-coloured dressings. Two canted bays with steep roofs and narrow, sharply-pointed dormer windows are joined by an arcade of marble pillars with freestone arches and elaborate Corinthian capitals; the whole two-storeyed, well-contained and gracing its splendid position. Past its entrance gates, the road to *Crogennen Lakes* carries traffic precariously by twisting gradients, with many gates to open, to the high plateau where the lakes, renowned for fishing, brood in desolate scenery against the massive background of Tyrau Mawr, part of the Cader Idris range. Then the road gets easier to join a better road running east to Dolgellau. The walk from Barmouth to the top of Cader Idris, by way of the estuary bridge, Arthog, the Crogennen Lakes, and Tyrau Mawr is not now as popular as it used to be in Norfolk jacket days.

Llangower (5). A small sparsely populated parish, rising into the hills south of Lake Bala. An indifferent road keeps company with the railway line along the lakeside. On it the church of St Cywair is a primitive, single chamber of rough grey stone, last restored in 1871. It has early, flat tombstones and the oldest yew tree in the county in the large bare churchyard. A brass coffin plate inside the church to Rowland Hugh (poet) of Graienyn is matched by another on a tombstone outside the south wall. On the south wall hangs a horse-drawn bier, similar to the one in Llangelynin. *Graienyn* is a small Georgian house on the hillside with fine lake and mountain views.

Further towards Bala, *Fach Ddeiliog* is a low bow-fronted house with recent and well composed extensions. As a motel, it has separate accommodation and is also the club house of the Bala Golf Club (nine-hole course).

Llansantffraid Glyndyfrdwy (3). A tiny parish the shape of an old unlaced boot, the toe dipping into the Dee at *Carrog,* a terraced village, which was once the principal domain of the Glyndwr family. Its best feature is a picturesque old bridge of five arches with cutwaters over the Dee. A new church of St Bride was built uphill from the flood level of the Dee in 1611 on the simple bellcote plan and restored in 1852; the chancel was added in 1865. The oak roof rafters may well have come from the earlier church. The heavy iron-studded doors and the round font certainly did.

Llanuwchllyn (5). The village at the western end of Lake Bala is compact and colourless; at its northern entrance, the head and torso statue on a round pillar of Sir Owen Morgan Edwards (1858–1920) as a youth; he was first Inspector of Schools for Wales. Its railings are thin metal outlines of human figures, a typical touch of Welsh eccentricity. Humiliated in boyhood by the English village schoolmaster, Edwards became a staunch advocate of the teaching of Welsh. Also to his memory is the wrought iron gate to the Methodist Cemetery, where he is buried. The gate, which turns on a central swivel, symbolises the Resurrection, and was designed by R. Gapper of Aberystwyth University. Beautifully wrought, it is the work of David J. Williams (d. 1966) of Caernarvon, who made and fitted the handles for the coffin of the Unknown Warrior. He was chosen by the Ministry of Public Building and Works to repair the famous gates of Chirk Castle, made by Robert Davies of Wrexham about two hundred years ago. His work is also in the Admiralty Board Room, Merton College Oxford, and Carisbrooke Castle. The village pump (Coalbrookdale cast iron) commemorates the birth in 1891 of Sir Watkin Williams Wynn, Bart; the village

school, built in 1841 on the coming of age of a previous Sir Watkin, is now a cottage. The Williams Wynn family, of Wynnstay, Ruabon, owned so much land in north Wales that they were known as the Princes in Wales. Their local seat *Glanllyn,* a double bow fronted, stone house of two storeys, overlooks Bala lake and is now used by *Urdd Gobaith Cymru* (The Welsh League of Youth) for summer camps.

The estate was transferred to the Treasury in 1944 on the death of the 7th baronet. It included the lake, the longest privately-owned water in Wales. In the village, the simple bellcote church of St Deinol was rebuilt in 1873 (architect E. B. Ferrey). A date, 1725, is scratched on a lychgate stone. The church is uninteresting but has an effigy of a knight in armour in the north wall of the sanctuary, and in the south aisle, a large chest used in the last century for baptism by immersion.

South from the parish, a narrow road follows the eastern slope of the *Cynllwyd* valley with westward views of lonely sheep farms. Beyond a hamlet at *Talardd* (small whitewashed chapel) it crosses a mountain pass to drop suddenly a thousand feet or so into the upper reaches of the *Dyn* valley. West of the village there are old gold workings on craggy *Castell Carndochau* and, beyond, in the shadow of the larches of *Coed Wenallt,* is the tiny Congregational *Carmel* chapel (1839–93), stone-built and gable-fronted. The lane is narrow, its verges strewn with boulders and within sound of tumbling water.

Caergai, a 17th-century manor house on the north slope of the main road out of Bala, is a two-storeyed, lattice-windowed house with a recessed centre. An earlier house was destroyed in the Civil War. Each wing has a stone slab with carved Welsh verses by the 17th-century poet Rowland Vaughan. Excavations in a field here in 1965 revealed the foundations of a Roman fort; the levelled ground on which the house now stands was its main part.

Llanycil (2). The ecclesiastical parish of Bala. The simple church of St Beuno, on the north side of Bala Lake in a profusion of yew trees and grave-stones, has been much restored,

but the 18th-century altar rails remain, as do many 18th- and early 19th-century tablets to Lloyd and Lloyd Anwil families. The railed grave of the revivalist Thomas Charles is near the east wall. Opposite the church entrance gabled cottage of 1838, a rectory, a village school and a rather dilapidated barn form a pleasant group.

The parish stretches far to the north into the slopes of the Snowdonia National Park. The fine Bala to Ffestiniog road skirts the recent *Treweryn holding reservoir,* also known as *Llyn Celyn*. Its purpose is to control the volume of water in the Dee, into which the Treweryn river flows at Bala. It was built by the Liverpool Corporation in a submerged valley under the landscape direction and design of Sir Frederick Gibberd. The conventional view is that this man-made lake, receding from the dam to follow the natural contours of the valley to its northern inlet, fits well into the landscape and is an improvement on the expanse of rocks and rushes of the clodded terrain that lies beneath it. It may be ungracious to suggest that this sheet of water has unnaturally cut down the surrounding hills and that the splendid black velvet road does not accord with the harsh boulder strewn slopes. Some houses and a chapel lie beneath the water. Liverpool Corporation has built a memorial chapel on the lake shore. This building, surmounted with a cross and rounded on its landward side, is intended to symbolise the coming to shore of the culture and religion of the drowned valley. Inside, the structure is of natural stone of different hues and textures, approached across an open verandah or deck; there is no seating. The bare floor is paved in slate and slate memorials on the wall list with simple dignity the names of those buried in the graveyard of Capel Celyn, followed by a couplet in Welsh by Ben Bowen, saying that here is found deep calm and a place to rest. The contrast with what has gone before is emphasised by the rough unmortared boulders of the old wall leading to the chapel and lake side.

At *Tyn y Bont* on the eastern approach to the reservoir there is a 20th-century chapel, in yellow, peel-

Pennant, LLANYMAWDDWY

ing paint, not without a structural personality.

The landscape is wild, craggy and sombre, saddened the more by the shells of deserted homesteads; enormous boulders jut out at the roadside; pylons bestride the land and their cables drape the sky. A side road back to Bala passes high, stone-walled sheep folds and a morose 1860 Methodist chapel at *Llidiardau*. Some six hundred feet above in the wilderness, ghostly *Llyn Arenig Fawr* has a legend of a farmer who found a calf in its rushes and from it bred a fine herd; one evening a little man playing on a pipe enticed the cattle into the lake which swallowed them up for ever. (*See also* Arenig.)

Llwynguril *see* **Llangelynin.**

Llanymawddwy (5). The feature of this remote parish on the eastern boundary is the spectacular road which climbs out of the Cowarch valley over Bwlch y Groes pass to join the Bala to Dolgellau road at Llanuwchllyn. Well-surfaced but narrow and with a precipitous verge, it pierces the Aran range and gives northward views of the Arenigs and beyond. The village is nothing more than a few houses but the church, dedicated to a local saint, Tydecho, is worth a visit. A small bellcote fabric with lancet windows well renewed in local slate, its charm is in its simplicity and in the contrast between the stark white interior walls and the Welsh inscription (*Thou art praised in Zion, O God*) painted above the high chancel arch in gold and red on a blue ground. Beyond, in the east window, is tender Victorian glass. An octagonal, early medieval font with scalloped edges rests on a heavy circular base. Jacobean communion table in vestry. Outside, low clipped yew trees edge the path from the 1958 gabled and stone-flagged lychgate, sympathetically designed in traditional style by P. M. Padmore.

Maentwrog (1). The village, in the Ffestiniog valley, was built early in the 19th century by William Oakeley, a pioneer of the slate industry. Of local stone throughout, it is a contrived, early Victorian beau ideal, more English than Welsh, of the garden village of a country seat, but one looks in vain for the twin lodges and the massive wrought iron gates; the Oakeley house, Tanybwlch, is on the other side of the valley, in Ffestiniog parish. The church of St Twrog, in the centre of the village, was rebuilt in a lofty alien style with a slate-hung western spire in 1896. Unplastered walls inside, an elaborate Oakeley memorial on the east wall, and paraffin lamps in circular chandeliers. The 1898 lychgate commemorates the sixty years of Queen Victoria's reign. Large old yew trees.

North of the entrance to the Trawsfynydd nuclear power station, a side road leads past slate-fenced fields to the Roman fort, *Tomen y mur*. This is a green mound on a rushy plateau, deserted except for a flanking forestry plantation. Near it is an earthwork, an amphitheatre, showing as an irregularity in the sheep cropped ground. The Romans were here from A.D. 78 to A.D. 140. Then the Normans, whose circular motte rises on the perimeter of the Roman camp. Lastly, the ruined farmstead of a more recent occupant with its gaping evisceration is to us the most poignant of the three stages.

Cynfal Fawr, off the Trawsfynydd to Ffestiniog road and west of Bont Newydd, is a notable, small manor house, typical of the pre-Georgian architecture of the county. Its 17th-century front has later and charming windows of triple, pointed panes in square frames under a dormered roof. The core is earlier and two massive cruck beams rise from ground level to join at the roof tree. Now a residential riding school, it was the home of Huw Llwyd (1533–1620) who soldiered in the Low Countries and whose return, unrecognised, to his native land and family, Thomas Love Peacock com-

memorates in *Headlong Hall* in this conversation between Huw and his sister

"Art thou a Welchman, old
    soldier, she cried.
Many years have I wandered, the
    stranger replied,
Twixt Danube and Thames many
    rivers there be,
But the bright waves of Cynfal
    are fairest to me."

His power as a bard is also remembered by a large rock on the bed of the Cynfal, known as *Huw Llwyd's Pulpit,* from which he is said to have declaimed. A stone plaque beside the door of the house commemorates in Welsh his grandson Morgan Llwyd (1619–59) as Puritan, Writer, Mystic and Author of *The Three Birds,* a dialogue in Welsh between the Eagle (Cromwell), the Dove (a Puritan) and the Raven (an Episcopalian).

For *Coedydd Maentwrog National Nature Reserve, see* Ffestiniog.

Mallwyd (8). The Dolgellau to Welshpool road branching east at Cross Foxes traverses fine bare country with the Aran range looming above, over the Oerddrws pass into the Cerist valley. There are two centres of population, Dinas Mawddwy and Mallwyd. *Dinas Mawddwy* once relied for its prosperity on the slate quarries developed by the Buckley family who built the *Plâs,* a large Victorian mansion, and surrounded it with specimen trees and rhododendrons. The quarries are now closed, Plâs demolished (after a fire) and Nature has control of all. The air of sadness about the village is not relieved by the three gabled chapels within a stone's throw of each other, built in 1867, 1868 and 1869. A brave, unaided effort towards alternative employment is being made by the *Meirion Woollen Mill,* the last in the county. Established in 1949 and housed in an old quarry building, it concentrates on Welsh flannels, tweeds and tapestry in modern and traditional designs. It took first and second prizes at the 1966 Royal Welsh Show. Another helpful feature of the village is the *Red Lion Hotel.* A band of 16th-century outlaws—the red-headed men of Mawddwy (Gwyll-

tion Cochion Mawddwy) is renowned in Welsh folklore. Ex-soldiers of the Wars of the Roses, they terrorised south Merioneth. Judge Owen of Dolgellau, ordered to suppress them, met his death at their hands. Their memory is also kept alive by the *Brigands Inn* at *Mallwyd,* a tall slate-hung 18th-century building with sash windows, favoured by anglers. Its rather gaunt exterior is not out of keeping with the associations of its name.

Mallwyd is trim and contained, with a distinct feeling of nearby Montgomeryshire, even of England. The parish church (dedicated to a local saint, Tydecho) has an interesting but unprepossessing Montgomeryshire-type tower, a wooden slatted belfry on a stone foundation. It was much restored in 1914, when the roof rafters over the nave were exposed and tiers of choir stalls were grouped below the organ at the west end. Memorial on south wall to Dr John Davies, author of a Latin/Welsh dictionary and incumbent of Mallwyd, is by Solomon Gibson (1796–1866), a Liverpool sculptor. Hanging chromium heaters. The massive oak lintel of the south porch is dated 1641. Above it are the rib and skull of what is thought locally to have been a prehistoric animal, found in the neighbourhood.

Moelwyn (1). The mountain range in the north of the county, on the edge of the Snowdonia syncline west of Blaenau Ffestiniog. It is a fiercely contorted landscape in which man's surface scratchings—the quarries now mostly abandoned, the heaps of slate spoil and the derelict homes of quarrymen—are reduced to insignificance by the convulsions and pressures of nature. The conical-looking top of *Cnicht,* on the county boundary, overlooks the Croesor valley and is easily reached from Croesor village (*see* Llanfrothen). But to the west of the range, the high ground slopes south-west towards the vale of Ffestiniog, over an expanse of grassland, skirted by the mountain road from Croesor to Tanybwlch. It is a fairly easy walk of a mile or so across this open stretch to the rocks at the foot of either Moelwyn Mawr

or Moelwyn Bach. Another route, and to the summit of these immense crags, known to rock climbers for over fifty years, is from the village of Croesor along the old slate-carrying tramway running north-east; near the northern spur of Moelwyn Mawr, old mine shafts present hazards and it is hard going southward to the mountain peak.

The whole of this wild terrain is pitted with lakes and old workings up to and beyond the county boundary. A more enduring monument to human endeavour, its dam clearly visible from the eastern approaches to Blaenau, is the *Central Electricity Generating Board* power station at *Llyn Stwlan*, a thousand feet above sea level, and the first of its kind in Britain. Water is pumped nightly from the lower man-made Tanygrisiau reservoir to the upper, natural, Llyn Stwlan and released daily through the water turbines, generating electricity when the demand is high. Coach trips for sightseers run between Blaenau and the power station.

Pennal (7). The Dolgellau road winds along the western flank of the Dulas valley towards Corris. It is shaded on the west by scrub oak, followed by plantations of beech and larch with larger firs in the background. In the autumn the colours are superb. The southern road towards Towyn, opened in 1827, overlooks the Dovey estuary, backed by the Cardiganshire hills.

The village has low slate-built cottages and the walled circular enclosure of St Peter's church forms a central roundabout. The church was rebuilt in the classical style early in the 19th century on the open plan with a slate, hipped roof and gilded weathercock at the west end. It was restored in 1860. The square-headed windows of the single chamber are mostly of diamond tinted glass, but there is conventional 20th-century stained glass (Ward and Hughes) and rich Victorian glass (Holland and Holt, Warwick). Tablets are mainly to Thurston families of Talgarth (*see* Towyn) and include one of bronze with a reclining female figure in mid-19th-century dress. The most impos-

RHINOG: The Roman Steps

ing, 18th century, has four heads in relief of white marble on a darkly mottled background. Against the west wall are three ornate round-headed oak medallions, probably 18th century, carrying high relief and well executed carvings of male busts in antique Roman style. They were given to the church by Bishop Watkin Williams. Their history is unknown.

There are two imposing chapels in the village; one, Methodist, early 20th century, and the other earlier, Independent, gable fronted and classical in style, galleried and ornate inside. The principal house of the parish, *Pennal Towers,* north of the village, has been rebuilt. It is on high ground, screened by trees. There is nothing left of the Roman fort at *Cefn Gaer,* east of the village, established to guard the Dovey.

Penrhyndeudraeth (1). The ribbon development along the main Portmadoc road north of the Dwyryd estuary has a central village nucleus and no dearth of chapel architecture. The principal building is Holy Trinity church built in 1858 in a lofty style with a west crocketed spire. It is refreshingly simple and modern inside with plenty of light through clear glass windows on white and pale blue walls. Bertrand Russell spent the last years of his life and died here.

Portmeirion is the show place, a village designed and built by Clough Williams Ellis from 1926 onwards, inspired by the Italian Riviera. On a lovely, natural south-facing site sloping to the sea, and in a bower of trees, he set out to create a group of buildings fitted to the landscape with no pretence to a coherent style, as a lesson in architectural good manners. Colonnades, Watch Tower, Gothic, Classical and Baroque façades, Campanile, Belvedere and Grottoes combine happily with traditional Welsh cottages in this setting. Each building has been sited to the best advantage of natural slopes and heights with an unerring eye for its dramatic—and in some instances one might also say its bizarre—effect. The Welsh feeling for inventive adornment, seen at its humblest in the decoration, for instance, of a keystone with pieces of coloured glass, is here generously exploited. Much of the material in-

On RHINOG Fach:
p132 Llyn y bo and
the Rhobells
p133 above and below
Rhinog Fawr and Llyn Hywel

corporated in the buildings has been rescued from demolished buildings throughout Britain. There is resident accommodation and car parks for day visitors. *Castell Deudraeth,* a large castellated mansion and part of the Portmeirion nucleus, was enlarged into its present shape in the mid 19th century by a Pwllheli solicitor, Mr Williams.

Portmeirion see **Penrhyndeudraeth**

Rhinog (4). A mile or so inland and west of the village of Llanbedr the road forks, right into *Nantcol valley* and left to *Cwm Bychan*. Both lead to the foothills of the Rhinog range. From the road up the Nantcol valley, often overlooking it, are displayed all the characteristics of Merioneth upland country; the immediate views of the architecture of farm buildings, with rough boulders assembled without mortar or cement; the formation of the rocks and their polished, fissured faces; the peaty streams running through water meadows flecked with bog cotton; the narrow road gaps left in the punctuations of stone walls, lichens and stonecrop diversifying all. The more distant views are of the river cascading below, and at suitable seasons the smoke rising from Scouts' holiday camps; the many, old and well-built stone field walls threading and cross-threading in complex patterns and diverging purposefully to climb the mountain slopes. The valley widens at *Pont Cerrig* and a regular pattern of cultivation appears. Beyond Pont Cerrig the road ends at *Maes y Garnedd,* a low two-storied farmhouse, once the home of Oliver Cromwell's brother-in-law, the regicide John Jones.

The *Rhinogs, Fach* to the right and south, *Fawr* to the north, look dark and shapely from the enclave of the Nantcol farms. In fact, this is the best view of them as a pair, although the composition of them on the skyline from the Trawsfynydd-Dolgellau road across country to the east is also striking. At Maes y Garnedd the footpath up through the defile, *Drws Ardudwy,* begins; at first over swampy ground with the lower slopes of Rhinog Fach falling away in boul-

dered terraces like the terrain of an Italian mountain village. Beyond the defile's first ridge well defined steps, the gaps between them paved, are very like and no doubt of the same age (medieval) as the "Roman" steps of Cwm Bychan. Where the ground is flat stone causeways provide firm footing over the rills and swamps. The pathway gradually rises to the Bwlch, the saddle of the pass, and the mountain sides. Fawr on the left at first and then Fach, become steeper and more forbidding in aspect. The natural rock faces are castellated, columnar and sometimes regularly ridged. There is always the sound of water, and there are impressive sections of level, almost table-top-smooth stone slabs — glacier-smoothed. The vegetation is heather and at the head of the defile the route becomes bare and deserted, emerging over the saddle and down to the Forestry Commission plantations south of Trawsfynydd lake.

Llyn Hywel, at eighteen hundred feet, in the shadow of Rhinog Fach is the largest of the lakes that fill craters and crevices of the Rhinogs. It is best reached by way of the Nantcol Valley and the turning up to the farm Graig Isaf. From here, on the 700-foot contour line the rocky face of Rhinog Fach is clearly visible. From the farm a tractor trail, quite unsuitable for cars, leads through abandoned farm buildings, the stone structure of which can still be admired for the way in which the gable ends, rising from protruding boulders at the base, reach their apex in perfect symmetry without aid of mortar or cement. Beyond these lie manganese mine workings where strands of the ropeway still lie or clear the ground in their ascent, and where old shafts are tunnelled into the hillside, dark and dripping. The track skirts the shoulder of the old workings and beyond a series of low ridges deep in heather you come to the final one overlooking Hywel's small sister lake, a rushy tarn, *Perfeddau,* below the slopes of *y Llethr.* A scramble over an intervening ridge on a bearing with the peak of Rhinog Fach brings you to Hywel.

On the south side, where streams start their descent from the lake's green shallows to the lowland, the

shore is flat; but the smooth steep face of Rhinog Fach rises almost sheer from the other side, with screes between broken rockfaces. These can suggest the recumbent shape of a giant with legs wide apart; the whole place is full of images which give it a strong personality.

The return journey can be made down the slope towards Maes y Garnedd farm and then cutting to the left along sheep tracks, where they exist, through the heather, and over rough table-like outcrops to the line of the manganese trail. With luck you may flush a brace of grouse, which are not too rare in the Rhinogs. From the lakeside to the north you will see the obliquely regular strata lines of Rhinog Fawr, and if the uniform grey above the heather line is tiring there are glimpses far to the left of the sea and the blue haze over Cardigan Bay.

The road to *Cwm Bychan,* longer and much more frequented, passes through close country and is narrow and at holiday times vexatious, but though less open and verdant than Nantcol, its valley is full of landscape beauty, with the river more in evidence under woodland shade. It has, with Nantcol, a feeling and atmosphere similar to those in the valleys on the seaward side of the Lake District, especially the Duddon valley.

Cwm Bychan lake forms the head of the valley, bordered on the north side by the narrow road and on the south by the steep slopes of Craig y Saeth (Arrow Crag). Beyond it a car park provides for the relatively large number of visitors, anxious to see the *Roman steps*—not in fact Roman, but a medieval pack trail between the Rhinogs into the Eden valley. The steps begin where the footpath from the car park emerges from the rough ground, shaded by silver birches, rowans, and scrub oak. The steps are irregularly spaced, generally most in evidence where they are needed most and absent from the flat marshy places. On the ascent of *Bwlch Tyddiad,* the pass into the valley, it is easy to miss the best stretch immediately at the foot of Rhinog Fawr, but this is unmistakable on the return journey. Rarely exceeding two feet in width, at their best they are regularly laid with half-buried

kerbstones jutting out of the heather. The immense westward views amply repay the rather arduous scramble to the head of the Bwlch, where if you have time it is worth continuing down into the valley and climbing the hill to the left by one of the sheep tracks through the thick heather which is broken by enormous, flat boulders. From this ground there is a fine close view of the north-western flank of Rhinog Fawr as it gradually loses height towards Coed y Brenin Forest.

Rhobell (5). *Rhobell Fawr* at 2,400 feet is the highest point of a massif which rises above the Wnion valley and in the centre of Llanfachreth parish. Thanks to the Forestry Commission the road northward from Rhydymain can now be used by cars through and over the range into Cwm yr Allt Llwyd. But it is steep in places, and narrow, and enclosed as far as Caer-defaid and then through the plantations to Ty-newydd on the 1,600-foot contour line, where younger trees are growing; beyond them to the left Rhobell Fawr rises sharply. An open stretch of grassland lies between Rhobell Fawr and its neighbour *Dduallt* which on the analogy of the Rhinogs and Arenigs should be renamed Rhobell Fach.

Talsarnau (1). Much of the northern end of the parish was reclaimed from the sea in 1810 by the construction of a turf embankment across the marsh south of Traeth Bach, and, behind it, the railway line and main road were laid about the middle of the last century. Until then the church of St Michael at *Llanfihangel Traethu* stood on an island outcrop. Rebuilt in 1871 it is still a lonely place, accessible across fields with gates to open and, being locked, hardly worth the detour.

Glyn Clywarch, the Merioneth seat of Lord Harlech, is the most beautifully composed early Jacobean house in the county. Built in 1616 for William and Katherine Wynne, from whom the Ormsby-Gore family is descended, it overlooks the plain under the shelter of the wooded hills. The exterior, of large granite blocks in two storeys with mullioned and dormer windows, has toned down to a soft dark grey colour. Inside, it is rich in period decoration, and mantelpieces have armorial shields in high plaster relief, one flanked by Adam with pick and shovel and Eve with serpent and tree. Wings added to the 1616 free standing gatehouse in an 1870 restoration, faithfully reproduce the earlier style; the ground floor windows of the front of the house were renewed at the same time.

Another Jacobean country house overlooking a charming valley is *Maes y Neuadd*, now an hotel, and much restored.

Talyllyn (7). The deep valley cleft is part of the Bala fault, a geological fracture line. The lake, source of the Dysynni river, is well described by that sensitive fisherman, Frank Ward: "When sunlight and cloud play over Talyllyn with every delicate gradation of colour few can equal and none excel the combined grandeur and loveliness of this peaceful valley. The first glimpse on a fine spring morning from the head of the valley approaching from the Dolgellau side is alone compensation for a long journey. Far away are the sunbathed grey and purple mountain summits and in the deep oval of the valley lies Talyllyn, turquoise and gold in a setting of emerald, the surface ruffled here and there to glittering cobalt." The lakeside *Tyn y Cornel Hotel* was built in 1844 by Colonel Vaughan of Hengwrt.

The church of St Mary on the western edge of the lake is a primitive building. The sloping churchyard has two lych-gates, each with a round-headed arch; stone seats in one and wooden in the other; the upper entrance for use when the lower is flooded. Near the latter a cross marks the grave of a Scotswoman, Jenny Jones, who "was with her husband of the 23rd Royal Welch Fusiliers at the Battle of Waterloo and was on the field three days". The church interior, much restored in 1876, has a south transept divided from the nave by a Jacobean yew wood partition, formerly the front of a gallery removed in 1876. The nave roof is of primitive 13th century and earlier work, with tie beams and projecting dowels. The curved Tudor chancel

Slate quarries' steps at CORRIS
(*see* Talyllyn)

roof is boarded, and the panels carry rose paintings in alternate red and white. Twelve faces are painted where dividing lines intersect. Paraffin lamps, closely balustraded 17th-century communion rails, and rather crude Victorian glass in the three-light east window.

Corris is the chief centre of population, a slate-miners' village off the main Dolgellau/Machynlleth road. It is a steep place of chapels, cottages and farms, densely populated, now partly in decay. At *Braich Goch*, piles of discarded slates hang precariously above the road. The village church of The Holy Trinity was built about 1860. It is approached under an avenue of Douglas firs and has a rich Victorian east window.

For Talyllyn Railway see Towyn.

Towyn (7). Going north, the coast road comes to the edge of the Dovey estuary; then for eight miles it follows the shore to the farther outskirts of Aberdovey. A single-track railway keeps it company, popping in and out of cuttings through the lower rocks. The road is cut into the hillside, high enough to give views of sands and water within the ring of distant mountains. The estuary is long and wide but at the bar it narrows to a thousand yards, so that at high tide it looks land-locked. Not far beyond the bar at Aberdovey, flat land intervenes between the sea and the road and the grandeur is lost. A secondary road runs roughly parallel, less than a mile inland, through the mountain gorge of *Cwm Dyffryn* and over a pass with a gradient of one in five and hairpin bends; footpaths lead off to *Llyn Barfog*, the Bearded Lake (covered in reeds) and to the *Happy Valley*, beauty spots behind Aberdovey. *Talgarth* on the outskirts of Pennal is a substantial 18th-century country house of dressed stone of three storeys, its plainness relieved by moulded lintels above the well-spaced windows. An arched loggia, quadrant shaped, connects the main block with a two-storeyed wing. It is now a country hotel and caravan park. *Dyffryn Gwyn* farmhouse in Cwm Dyffryn valley has a 1640 date

stone. It is alongside a footpath behind a modern bungalow, and has a George Morland air.

Towyn has no natural features to give it extra character. It became a seaside place instead of an inland village, a mile or so from the sea, because of John Corbett, a salt magnate from Droitwich, where his enormous French Renaissance house, Chateau Impney, gives a clue to his character. In 1884 he bought Ynysmaengwyn estate on the outskirts of Towyn from the impoverished, unrelated Corbet family. In 1889 he built the fine sea wall esplanade, about half a mile long, and an imposing block of houses, *Marine Terrace*, at its northern end. But interest in it seems to have waned as the front is still undeveloped and bare, petering out at its southern end into a caravan park.

The town centre, Corbett Square, is small and has buildings of character; notably the *Corbett Arms Hotel*. Formerly the Corbet Arms it predates in its present form the arrival of John Corbett by about fifty years. Alternate pediments and curved hoods above the windows of the middle storey pleasantly break the flat, imposing façade, topped by eight dormer sash windows. The *Market Hall*, a John Corbett benefaction, is a well-composed low building of contrasting coloured stone, with a central clock tower and cupola and Dutch gables on its flank elevations. The prettiest building is the 1893 *Assembly Rooms*, now a cinema. Its main feature is an elaborate cast iron balcony opening from a large, round-headed central window under an arch carried up into the gable front. Urn finials in white picked out in red are supported on pedestals at each corner and on the gable point. The background colour is faded azure blue, the balcony white and the white cornice has red starfish-shaped decorations. Altogether very showy.

The parish church of St Cadfan, off Corbett Square, is a 12th-century foundation, cruciform, with a central tower. The latter was replaced on its original Norman foundations in an 1885 restoration, after it had been removed to the west end in the 18th century. The 1885 restoration rebuilt the transepts and east end and shortened the west end. Inside, it has

something for everybody; from the Dark Ages St Cadfan's stone, a four-sided pillar, probably 7th century, carries the first known inscription in Welsh, and two incised crosses. For the medievalist there are the heavy, round, unadorned pillars of the arcades below deeply-splayed clerestory windows and two 14th-century effigies in the north wall of the chancel, one of a knight of Dolgoch, Grufydd ap Adda, the other of a priest. The 18th century is well represented by a splendid Ynysmaengwyn tablet by Sir Henry Cheere. To bridge the gulf with the Victorian furniture, which includes an elaborately carved organ case, a bass viol from the old musicians gallery hangs on a chancel arch. The best 20th-century feature is a stained glass window by Geoffrey Webb in the chancel.

18th century and earlier cottage rows have either been demolished to make way for modern villas, or so altered externally as to be unrecognisable; but one early house, at the corner of National Street and Ffordd Cadfan, is worth looking at. Built of rough stones which stand out of their cement rendering like currants in a cake, it has dormer windows above the two storeys, heavy slate lintels and a central, round-headed window.

The revival of the Talyllyn two-foot-three-inch gauge railway which runs between Towyn and Abergynolwyn brings many enthusiasts to Towyn, its western terminus. Its history and rolling stock are well described in the local guide and the Company's Handbook. It was laid just over a hundred years ago to bring slates and possibly gold ore to the coast. There was no gold, and when the cost of getting slates became prohibitive the line languished until the Talyllyn Railway Preservation Society took it over in 1950. This was the first venture of its kind and its success, supported entirely from the Society's own resources and voluntary contributions, is measured by the one hundred and thirty-two thousand passengers carried in 1969, compared with eighty thousand in 1964. The Society's workshop is at Pendre, near Corbett Square. For further information write to the Traffic Manager, Wharf Station, Towyn.

TOWYN

The Dolgellau road from Towyn
passes the lodge gates of *Ynysmaengwyn*, notable Georgian house
of the Corbet family, now irre-
mediably decayed and in process of
demolition. It consisted of two
separate buildings, facing each other,
and each of three gabled bays, built
in the 1730s. In 1758 a large central
block in Classical style was added
and connected to the rest by two
curved loggias. It was not an attractive building externally, and its loss
is not deplorable. Beyond its park,
two valleys converge to the plain at

Bryn Crug—the Dysynni, forming
the parish boundary, and the Fathew
running up to Talyllyn Lake. *Bryn
Crug* has a simple 1880 church, dedicated to St Matthew, built by the
Wynne family of Peniarth in Llanegryn parish, and two chapels. The
Dysynni valley is a wide marsh
broken by clumps of trees with a
narrow outlet to the sea. It is crossed
by the main road and a lane follows
it to *Birds Rock*, which rises
to seven hundred and fifty feet above
the valley floor and is still a nesting
place for sea birds, including cor-

morants, although the sea is now
five miles or so away.

The Fathew valley road passes
Dolaugwyn, a Jacobean (1620) manor
house hardly touched by time, and
splendidly maintained. It can be seen
clearly from the road. External
features are the delicately coloured
grey stone, the central porch and
arched doorway, mullioned windows
and decoratively stepped gables.
Inside, the staircase is original, and
heraldic devices in the drawing room
and kitchen have 17th-century dates.
Beyond, the valley narrows, and its

138

lower slopes are richly wooded. At *Dolgoch* a viaduct on brick piers carries the Talyllyn Railway on its beautifully scenic course across a gorge of a mountain torrent, cascading through rocks and scrub oaks.

Trawsfynydd (1). There is a strong sense of the approaching slate-mining country about the hillside village, which contains nothing of interest except the church of St Madryn, and that has suffered from a mid 19th-century restoration. An arcade of wooden octagonal pillars divides the nave from a south chamber, added in the 16th century. Plenty of slate and brass memorials on the green walls, and tiered seats at the west end have been boarded off. An elaborate Victorian Gothic font, with a tall, spire shaped, wooden cover in Decorated style to match, has replaced the modest wooden font, perhaps early 18th century and now against the west wall. There is no chancel arch, and the best feature is the medieval roof over each chamber.

A fast, straight road on a north/south axis enters this vast bare parish north of *Coed y Brenin Forest* to a "western" film-set view of open Indian country, with the Rhinog range of table tops and peaks as a Wyoming background. On this wild background are two lakes which Frank Ward writes of as the most inaccessible in Wales, *Pryved* in a rocky hollow of **Craig Wion** and, a few hundred yards northward, *Twr Glas*. Since Ward's day the metalled road across the grassy plain by way of *Pont Gribble* to the outskirts of Coed y Brenin forest has brought these lakes nearer, but has in no way mitigated the rigours of the last stages of the journey, from the ruined farm of *Graigddu Uchaf* in the forest up the course of the stream which rises in Pryved. For the first few hundred yards it is not always possible to follow the stream and detours are necessary over thick, hussocky, knee-high grass in which narrow drainage dykes are hidden; a possible alternative is by the wide ride which leads westward out of the forest and round the forest boundary until the stream is met. From then on the way is arduous and dangerous because the thick, wiry heather conceals boulders and crevices, sometimes three feet deep, between them, so that a false step can easily result in a twisted ankle and the district is so remote that help is not at hand. As the climb gets steeper, so the boulders lie thicker and larger, and eventually they completely obscure the stream which can be heard flowing below them, underground and ominous in this desolate place. One is tempted to leave the stream and take a short cut to where one imagines Pryved to be, only to find that ridge conceals hostile ridge and one is forced back to the stream. Once reached, Pryved and Twr Glas are little more than tarns. Pryved is rushy at its southern end, narrow and boulder-edged. There is evidence that it is fished from the worn bank on the eastern side; perhaps the anglers have some quicker, secret route. All around the rocks have extraordinary shapes. Some have short columned ridges; boulders are balanced precariously on glacier rocks, and the way across to nearby Twr Glas is like traversing an ice floe, so huge are the flat smooth rock surfaces. Twr Glas is on the very edge of a plateau; below, glitters *Trawsfynydd Lake* and to the north-east on the sky line there are the curious terraced slopes of *Craig Ddrwg*. The two-and-a-half-inch Ordnance Survey map shows many hut circles hereabouts, but they cannot be discerned at ground level. There are the rough remains of a prehistoric burial chamber with a tilted capstone on the slopes south-east of Pryved. Because of the rough terrain the return journey is hardly less difficult.

Branaber is an untidy wayside collection of corrugated iron, and abandoned war-time emplacements, but it is soon passed and the nuclear power station and its lake comes into view. Designed by Sir Basil Spence, its twin rectangular masses neither offend nor enhance the landscape; a nearer view exposes its rawness. The lake, three miles long and best seen from the slopes of the Rhinogs to the south-west, was formed by impounding the waters of the streams flowing into the valley from the south-east.

Maps

Map 1: Cardiganshire

Map 2: Merioneth

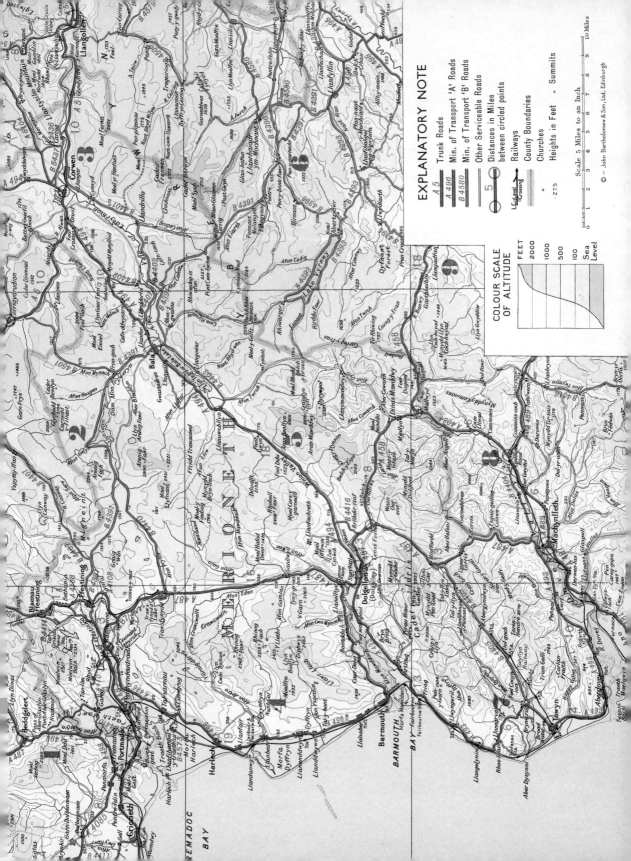

EXPLANATORY NOTE

A 5	Trunk Roads
A 496	Min. of Transport 'A' Roads
B 4580	Min. of Transport 'B' Roads
	Other Serviceable Roads
5	Distances in Miles between circled points
	Railways
Level Crossing	
	County Boundaries
+	Churches
.275	Heights in Feet
▲	Summits

Scale 5 Miles to an Inch

0 1 2 3 4 5 6 7 8 9 10 Miles

© – John Bartholomew & Son, Ltd, Edinburgh

COLOUR SCALE OF ALTITUDE

FEET
2000
1000
500
100
Sea Level

Index

(C) *indicates Cardiganshire section,* (M) *Merioneth. Lakes are shown by prefix Llyn, e.g. for Lake Hywel see Llyn Howel.*

Aberbanc, hamlet and chapel, *see* Orllwyn (C)

Aber Ceiro Fach, cottage, *see* Cwmrheidol (C)

Aberceri, house, *see* Brongwyn (C)

Aberffrwd, hamlet, *see* Melindwr (C)

Abergwesin Mountain Road, *see* p. 10 (C), Tregaron (C)

Abergynolwyn, village, *see* Llanfihangel y Pennant (M)

Aberhirnant Forest, *see* Llandderfel (M)

Abermad House, *see* Llanychaearn (C)

Abermeurig Hall, *see* Gartheli (C)

Abernant, hamlet, *see* Llanbadarn y Creuddyn Upper (C)

Admiralty Board Room, *see* Llanuwchllyn (M)

Aeron, river, *see* p. 9 (C), Aberaeron (C), Gwynfil (C)

Afon Lliw, *see* p. 78 (M)

Agriculture, *see* p. 19 (C)

Alex Gordon and Partners, architects, *see* Lampeter (C)

Alltyrodin, house, *see* Llandyssul (C)

Alwen, river, *see* Llangar (M)

Andrews, Solomon, *see* Llangelynin (M)

Angler's Retreat, house, *see* Ceulany Maes Mawr (C)

Architecture: domestic, *see* p. 26 (C), pp. 88, 90 (M); civic, *see* p. 90 (M); church and chapel, *see* pp. 26, 28 (C), pp. 90, 91 (M)

Arthog, village, *see* Llangelynin (M)

Art Nouveau, *see* Brithdir (M)

Artro, river and valley, *see* Llanbedr (M), Llanfair (M)

Asturian Cohort, *see* Llanddewi Brefi (C)

Atkin, Baron James Richard, *see* Aberdovey (M)

Baily, E. H., sculptor, *see* Llanbadarn Fawr (C), Dolgellau (M)

Baker and Hughes, architects, *see* Ystrad Meurig (C)

Baker, James, (*Guide through Wales*), *see* Ciliau Aeron (C)

Bala Fault, *see* p. 78 (M), Talyllyn (M)

Baldwin, Thomas, architect, *see* Llanfihangel y Creuddyn Upper (C)

Bangor, hamlet, *see* Orllwyn (C)

Bardsey Island, *see* Llandanwg (M)

Barlow, sculptor, *see* Llangoedmor (C)

Basque Churches, *see* Llanaber (M)

Beaver, last haunt of, *see* p. 9 (C)

Belgian woodcarvers, *see* Llanfihangel y Creuddyn Lower (C), Llanwenog (C)

Bell, Sir H. Idris (*The Development of Welsh Poetry*), *see* Llanbadarn Fawr (C)

Belloc, Hilaire (*The Cruise of the Non*), *see* p. 82 (M)

Benares, making of ice in, *see* Troedyraur (C)

Bendigo, racehorse, *see* Llanfor (M)

Benedictine Order, *see* Cardigan (C), Llanbadarn Fawr (C)

Benllyn, *see* Aran (M)

Bernaerts, Jules, woodcarver, *see* Llanfihangel y Creuddyn Lower (C)

Berwyn, river, *see* Tregaron (C)

Bethania, chapel, *see* p. 28 (C) Cardigan (C), hamlet *see* Cilcennin (C)

Bethel, chapels, *see* Ceulany Maes Mawr (C) Llanegryn (M), hamlet, *see* Llandderfel (M)

Bethesda, chapel, *see* Llandygwydd (C)

Bettws Bledrws, *see* Llangybi (C)

Beyer Peacock and Co., locomotive builders, *see* Llandderfel (M)

Birds' Rock, *see* Llanfihangel y Pennant (M)

Black Lion Hotel, *see* Ceulany Maes Mawr (C)

Black, (*Guide to Wales*), *see* Plinlimon (C)

Blaenannerch, hamlet and chapel, *see* Aberporth (C)

Blaenau Ffestiniog, *see* Ffestiniog (M)

Blaencwm, hamlet, *see* Llanfihangel y Creuddyn Upper (C), farm, *see* Llandrillo (M)

Blaendyffryn, house, *see* Orllwyn (C)

Blaenpant, house, *see* p. 26 (C), Llandygwydd (C)

Blake, Capt. R. N., tablet, *see* Corwen (M)

Bodweni Hall, *see* Llandderfel (M)

Bontddu, *see* pp. 80, 85 (M), Llanaber (M)

Bont Goch, hamlet, *see* Tirymynach (C)

Borrow, George, Hotel, *see* Cwmrheidol (C)

Boston, New England, Ann Jones tombstone, *see* Llanbadarn Fawr (C)

Bouchier family, *see* Corwen (M)

Bowen, Ben, *see* Llanycil (M)

Bow Street, village, *see* Tirymynach (C)

Braich Goch, *see* Talyllyn (M)

Branaber, hamlet, *see* Trawsfynydd (M)

Bremia, (Loventium), *see* Llanddewi Brefi (C)

Brigands Inn, *see* Mallwyd (M)

Brithdir, hamlet, *see* Penbryn (C)

British and Foreign Bible Society, *see* Llanfihangel y Pennant (M)

Broad Water, *see* Llangelynin (M)

Brongest, hamlet, *see* Troedyraur (C)

Bronwydd, house, *see* p. 26 (C), Llangynllo (C)

Bronze Age, *see* p. 13 (C), p. 77 (M), cairns, *see* Llanfair Clydogau (C), Llanenddwyn (M), bucket, *see* Llanfachreth (M), hoard, *see* Cader Idris (M)

Bryn Crug, *see* Towyn (M)

Bryn Hirfaen, *see* Cellan (C)

Bryn Mawr, *see* Llanfair Clydogau (C)

Brynyreithin, house, *see* Llanychaearn (C)

Building material, *see* p. 13 (C), p. 88 (M)

Butterfield, William, architect, *see* p. 26 (C), Aberystwyth (C), Ceulany Maes Mawr (C), Llangorwen (C)

Burgess, Bishop Thomas, *see* Lampeter (C)

Bwlchllan, hamlet, *see* Nantcwnlle (C)

Bwlch Tyddiad, *see* Rhinog (M)

Bwlch y Groes, *see* Llanymawddwy (M)

Byron, Lord, *see* Llanbadarn y Creuddyn Lower (C)

Cadair Berwyn, *see* Berwyn (M)

Cadair Bronwen, *see* Berwyn (M)

Cae Peris Farm, *see* Aran (M)

Caer Berllan, house, *see* Llanfihangel y Pennant (M)

Caer Defaid, *see* Rhobell (M)

Caerdeon, house, *see* Llanaber (M)

Caer Drewyn, *see* p. 78 (M)

Caergai, house, *see* Llanuwchllyn (M)

Caernwch Hall, *see* Brithdir (M), Dolgellau (M)

Calvinistic Methodism, *see* Llangeitho (C), Bala (M)

Camddwr, river, *see* Tregaron (C)

Camlan, stream, *see* Llanelltud (M)

Capel Bangor, village, *see* Llanfihangel y Creuddyn Upper (C), Melindwr (C)

Capel Celyn, *see* Llanycil (M)

Capel Cynon, hamlet, *see* Llantyssiliogogo (C)

Capel Dewi, hamlet, *see* Llandyssul (C)

Capel Seion, hamlet, *see* Llanbadarn y Creuddyn Upper (C)

Capel Vicar, hamlet, *see* Llanarth (C)

Caracci, Annibaele, artist, *see* Lampeter (C)

Cardigan Island, *see* Verwick (C)

Carisbrooke Castle, *see* Llanuwchllyn (M)

Carmel, chapels, *see* Llanilar (C), Llanuwchllyn (M)

Caröe, W. D., architect, *see* Llanfihangel y Creuddyn Upper (C)

Caron is Clawd, parish, *see* Tregaron (C)

Caron uwch Clawd, parish, *see* Pont-rhydfendigaid (C)

Carpenters Arms Inn, *see* Llangoedmor (C)

Carrog, hamlet, *see* Llansantffraid Glyndwfrdwy (M)

Castell Carndochau, gold workings, *see* Llanuwchllyn (M)

Castell Deudraeth, house, *see* Penrhyndeudraeth (M)

Castell Gwalter, *see* Llandre (C)

Castell Humphrey or Hywel, *see* Llandyssul (C)

Castell y Bere, *see* Llanfihangel y Pennant (M)

Castiglione, Professor G., *see* Dolgellau (M)

Castle Hill, house, *see* Llanilar (C)

Castle House, *see* Aberystwyth (C)

Cefn Gaer, *see* p. 78 (M) Pennal (M)

Cefn Quarries, *see* p. 88 (M), Llandderfel (M), Corwen (M)

Ceiriog Valley, *see* Llandderfel (M)

Celtic Studios, stained glass, *see* Borth (C), Llanfair Clydogau (C), Llangeitho (C), Silian (C), Tregaron (C), Llandanwg (M)

Cenarth, *see* p. 9 (C), Llandygwydd (C)

Central Electricity Boards, *see* Llanbadarn y Creuddyn Upper (C), Moelwyn (M)

Central School of Design, London, *see* Brithdir (M)

Ceri, valley and river, *see* Bettws Ifan (C), Brongwyn (C)

Cerist Valley, *see* Mallwyd (M)

Ceulan Valley, *see* p. 9 (C), Ceulan y Maes Mawr (C)

Challenger, lifeboat, *see* Llanfor (M)

Chantrey, sculptor, *see* Llanfihangel y Creuddyn Upper (C)

Charles, Rev. Thomas, *see* Bala (M), Llanfihangel y Pennant (M), Llanycil (M)

Chateau Impney, *see* Towyn (M)

Cheere, Sir Henry, sculptor, *see* Towyn (M)

Chirk Castle, *see* Llanuwchllyn (M)

Cilbronnau, house, *see* Llangoedmor (C)

Cilgerran, ravine, *see* p. 9 (C), Llangoedmor (C), slate, *see* Cardigan (C)

Cilgwyn, house, *see* Llandyfriog (C)

Cistercian Order, *see* Llanbadarn Fawr (C), Llanfihangel Ystrad (C), Pontrhydfendigaid (C), Llanelltud (M)

Clarach, *see* Llangorwen (C)

Clark, Lindsay, sculptor, *see* Lampeter (C)

Clayton and Bell, stained glass, *see* Verwick (C)

Clettwr Valley, *see* p. 9 (C), Ceulan y Maes Mawr (C)

Cletwr Valley, *see* Llandyssul (C)

Clogau, gold mine, *see* Llanaber (M)

Clwedog, stream, *see* Dolgellau (M)

Clwyd, Vale of, *see* p. 81 (M), river, *see* Gwyddelwern (M)

Cnicht, *see* Llanfrothen (M), Moelwyn (M)

Cnwch Goch (hamlet), *see* Llanfihangel y Creuddyn Lower (C)

Cockerell, C. R., architect *see* p. 26 (C), Lampeter (C), Llanbadarn y Creuddyn Lower (C), Llangybi (C)

Coed Llyn y Garnedd, *see* Moelwyn (M)

Coedmor, house, *see* Llangoedmor (C)

Coed Wenallt, *see* Llanuwchllyn (M)

Coed y Brenin Forest, *see* Llanddwywe Uwch y Graig (M), Llanfachreth (M), Rhinog (M), Trawsfynydd (M)

Coedydd Maentwrog National Nature Reserve, *see* Ffestiniog (M)

Coleg Harlech, *see* Llandanwg (M)

Constitution Hill, *see* Aberystwyth (C)

Continental Atmosphere, *see* p. 28 (C), Aberaeron (C), Cardigan (C)

Coracles, *see* pp. 9, 13 (C), Llandygwydd (C)

Corbet Family, *see* Towyn (M)

Corbett Arms Hotel, *see* Towyn (M)

Corbett, John, *see* Towyn (M)

Correggio, artist, *see* Lampeter (C)

Corris, village, *see* Talyllyn (M)

Cors y Gedol, house, *see* Llanddwywe is y Graig (M)

Court House, *see* Cardigan (C)

Coventry Education Committee, *see* Ffestiniog (M)

Cowarch Valley, *see* Aran (M), Llanymawddwy (M)

Cox, David, artist, *see* Lampeter (C)

Crafnant, farm, *see* Llanfair (M)

Craig Aderyn, or Birds' Rock, *see* Llanfihangel y Pennant (M), Towyn (M)

Craig Ddrwg, *see* Trawsfynydd (M)

Craig Wion, *see* Trawsfynydd (M)

Craig y Dinas, *see* p. 78 (M)

Craig yr Hyrddwd, *see* Arenig (M)

Craig y Saeth, *see* Rhinog (M)

Crescent, cottages, *see* Llangelynin (M)

Croesor, village, *see* Llanfrothen (M), Moelwyn (M)

Croft Castle, Ludlow, *see* Llanfihangel y Creuddyn Upper (C)

Crogen, house, *see* Llandderfel (M)

Crogennen Lakes, *see* Llangelynin (M)

Cromwell, Thomas, *see* Llandderfel (M)

Cross Foxes Inn, *see* Brithdir (M), Mallwyd (M)

Cross Inn, *see* Pontrhydfendigaid (C)

Crosswood, house, *see* Llanafan (C)

Cunedda, *see* p. 77 (M) Cader Idris (M)

Cunobelinus, King, *see* Llancynfelin (C)

Cwm Bychan, *see* Rhinog (M)

Cwmcoy, hamlet, *see* Brongwyn (C)

Cwmcynfelin, house, *see* Llangorwen (C)

Cwm Dyffryn, *see* Towyn (M)

Cwm Moch, *see* p. 78 (M)

Cwmtudu, hamlet, *see* Llantyssiliogogo (C)

Cwrt Newydd, hamlet, *see* Llanwenog (C)

Cyfrwy, *see* Cader Idris (M)

Cymmer Abbey, *see* Llanelltud (M)

Cynfal Fawr, house, *see* Maentwrog (M)

Cynfal, river, *see* Maentwrog (M)

Cynllwyd Valley, *see* Llanuwchllyn (M)

Cynwydd, village, *see* Llangar (M)

Dafydd ap Gwilym, poet, *see* Llanbadarn Fawr (C), Pontrhydfendigaid (C)

Dark Ages, legends of, *see* p. 13 (C)

Darwin, Bernard, *see* Aberdovey (M)

Davies, David of Llandinam, *see* Aberystwyth (C)

Davies, David, translator, *see* Llandyssul (C)

Davies, Elidir, architect, *see* Lampeter (C)

Dduallt, *see* Rhobell (M)

Dee, river, *see* p. 81 (M), Llandderfel (M), Llangar (M), Llansantffraid Glyndwfrdwy (M), Llanycil (M)

Deheubarth, Kingdom of, *see* p. 77 (M)

Depopulation figures, *see* p. 19 (C)

Derry Ormond, house, *see* p. 26 (C), Llangybi (C)

Devil's Bridge, *see* Llanfihangel y Creuddyn Upper (C)

Dinas Mawddwy, *see* Mallwyd (M)

Dr Williams School for Girls, *see* Dolgellau (M), Llanaber (M)

Dolaugwyn, house, *see* Towyn (M)

Dolddeuli Farm, *see* Aran (M)

Doleinion Guest House, *see* Cader Idris (M)

Dolgoch, *see* Towyn (M)

Dolmelynllyn Hall, *see* Llanelltud (M)

Dolmens, absence of, *see* p. 13 (C), site, *see* p. 77 (M), Llanenddwyn (M)

Dolrhyd, house, *see* Dolgellau (M)

Dolybont, hamlet, *see* Llandre (C)

Dolymoch, house, *see* Ffestiniog (M)

Douglas and Fordham, architects, *see* Barmouth (M)

Douglas, John, architect, *see* Bettws Gwerfil Goch (M)

Dovey Hotel, *see* Aberdovey (M)

Dovey, river, *see* p. 85 (M), Pennal (M)

Drefach, hamlet, *see* Llanwenog (C)

Drovers trails, *see* p. 10 (C)

Drws Ardudwy, *see* Rhinog (M)

Drws Bach, *see* Aran (M)

Drws y Nant Station, *see* Aran (M)

Dudley Arms Hotel, *see* Llandrillo (M)

Dulas Valley, *see* Pennal (M)

Dwyryd estuary, *see* Penrhyndeudraeth (M)

Dyffryn Ardudwy, village, *see* p. 77 (M), Llanenddwyn (M)

Dyffryn Bern Farm, tumulus and inscribed stone, *see* Penbryn (C)

Dyffryn Castle Hotel, *see* p. 11 (C)

Dyffryn Gwyn Farm, *see* Towyn (M)

Dyffwys Mountains, *see* Llanddwywe is y Graig (M)

Dyn Valley, *see* Llanuwchllyn (M)

Dysynni, river and valley, *see* p. 85 (M), Llanfihangel y Pennant (M), Llangelynin (M), Talyllyn (M), Towyn (M)

Ebenezer, chapels, *see* Barmouth (M), Llanegryn (M)

Eden Valley, *see* Llanfachreth (M), Rhinog (M)

Edeyrnion, vale of, *see* p. 81 (M)

Edinburgh Academy, *see* Ystrad Meurig (C)

Edward, Duke of Windsor, *see* Llandanwg (M)

Edward, I King, *see* p. 77 (M)

Edwards, Dr Lewis, *see* Bala (M)

Edwards, Sir Owen Morgan, *see* Llanuwchllyn (M)

Eglwys Fach, village, *see* Ysgubor Coed (C)

Egryn Abbey, *see* Llanaber (M)

Einion Valley, *see* p. 9 (C), Ceulany Maes Mawr (C)

Eisteddfa Gurig, *see* Cwmrheidol (C)

Elerch, village, *see* Ceulany Maes Mawr (C)

Elim Four Square Gospel Church, *see* Aberystwyth (C)

Ellis, T.E., M.P., *see* Bala (M)

English Services in Wales Act, *see* Llanaber (M)

Evans, Caradoc, writer, *see* Troedyraur (C)

Evans, Dr. Eifion, (*The Welsh Revival of 1904*), *see* Aberporth (C)

Fach Ddeiliog, house and motel, *see* Llangower (M)

Fainc-ddu rocks, *see* Plinlimon (C)

Fairbourne, village, *see* Llangelynin (M)

Falcondale, house, *see* Lampeter (C)

Falcon Inn, *see* Llanilar (C)

Farms, acreage and economy of, *see* p. 19 (C)

Fathew Valley, *see* Towyn (M)

Fegla Fawr Farm, *see* Llangelynin (M)

Felindre, hamlet, *see* Llanfihangel Ystrad (C)

Felin Fawr, house, *see* Llandre (C)

Felin Newydd (Central Electricity Board) *see* Llanbadarn y Creuddyn Upper (C)

Felin Ucha, mill, *see* Llangar (M)

Ferrey, Benjamin, architect, *see* p. 91 (M), Bala (M), Llanfachreth (M), Llanfor (M), Llanuwchllyn (M)

Ferguson, C. J., architect, *see* Aberystwyth (C)

Festiniog Railway Society, *see* Ffestiniog (M)

Ffair Rhos, *see* Pontrhydfendigaid (C)

Ffestiniog, vale of, *see* p. 85 (M)

Ffordd Gam Elin, *see* Berwyn (M)

Ffrwyd y Camddwr, *see* Tregaron (C)

Fish and Anchor Inn, *see* Lampeter (C)

Fitzwilliam family, *see* Llandyfriog (C)

Flaxman, sculptor, *see* Llanbadarn Fawr (C)

Fleure, Professor H. J., (*The Natural History of Man*), *see* p. 13 (C)

Florence, St. Mark's Church, *see* Brithdir (M)

Fonthill, *see* Llanfihangel y Creuddyn Upper (C)

Ford Madox Ford, (*The Fifth Queen*), *see* Llandderfel (M)

Forest, Father, martyr, *see* Llandderfel (M)

Forestry Commission, *see* p. 11 (C), Llanddewi Brefi (C), Llanfair Clydogau (C), Pontrhydfendigaid (C) Aran (M), Llanfachreth (M), Llanfrothen (M), Llanddwywe uwch y Graig (M), Rhinog (M), Rhobell (M)

Fowler, F., architect, *see* Ciliau Aeron (C)

Foxes Path, *see* Cader Idris (M)

Franceys, S. and F, sculptors, *see* Llanfachreth (M)

Friog Rocks, *see* Llangelynin (M)

Fron Goch, pool, *see* Llanfihangel y Creuddyn Upper (C), hamlet, *see* Llanfor (M)

Furnace, hamlet, *see* Ysgubor Coed (C)

Fuseli, artist, *see* Llanfihangel y Creuddyn Upper (C)

Gaer Fawr, hillfort, *see* p. 13 (C), Llanafan (C)

Gaffin, T., sculptor, *see* Llanfachreth (M)

Ganllwyd, hamlet, *see* Llanddwywe uwch y Graig (M), valley, *see* Llanelltud (M), Llanfachreth (M)

Gapper, R., *see* Llanuwchllyn (M)

Garreg Fawr, monument, *see* Llanfachreth (M)

Gatehouses, *see* p. 88 (M), Llanddwywe is y Graig (M), Llanfor (M), Talsarnau (M)

Gelli Deg, *see* Arenig (M)

Geneu yr Glyn, parish, *see* Llandre (C)

Geology, *see* p. 13 (C), p. 78 (M)

George III, King, *see* Bala (M), Llanfachreth (M)

George III Hotel, *see* Brithdir (M)

George IV, King, *see* Lampeter (C)

Gernos, house, *see* Llangynllo (C)

Gibberd, Sir Frederick, architect, *see* Llanycil (M)

Gibbs, Alexander, stained glass, *see* Barmouth (M)

Gibson, Solomon, sculptor, *see* Mallwyd (M)

Gilbert Marshall, Norman warlord, *see* Cardigan (C)

Gilbertson, Jane, tablet, *see* Llancynfelin (C)

Ginn Bros, organ makers, *see* Llanegryn (M)

Glanarberth, house, *see* Llangoedmor (C)

Glandwr, house, *see* Penbryn (C)

Glandyfi Castle, *see* Ysgubor Coed (C)

Glanllyn, house, *see* Llanuwchllyn (M)

Glan Medeni, house, *see* Bettws Ifan (C)

Glanolmarch, house, *see* Llangoedmor (C)

Glan yr Afon, hamlet and church, *see* Llandderfel (M)

Glan y Mawddach, house, *see* Llanaber **(M)**

Glasby, William, stained glass, *see* Llangoedmor (C)

Glasffrwyd Valley, *see* p. 11 (C), Pontrhydfendigaid (C)

Glenarthen, chapel and school, *see* Penbryn (C)

Glendower, *see* under Owain Glyndwr

Goedol, stream, *see* Ffestiniog (M)

Gogerddan, house and family, *see* Llanbadarn Fawr (C), Trefeirig (C)

Goginan, village, *see* Melindwr (C)

Goldmines, *see* Llanaber (M), Llanfachreth (M), Llanuwchllyn (M)

Goodhart-Rendel, *see* p. 28 (C), Lampeter (C)

Gorsgoch, hamlet, *see* Llanwenog (C)

Graienyn, house, *see* Llangower (M)

Graigddu Uchaf Farm *see* Trawsfynydd (M)

Graig Issaf Farm, *see* Rhinog (M)

Great Desert of Wales, *see* p. 10 (C), Tregaron (C)

Greenslade, S. K., architect, *see* Aberystwyth (C)

Grey, Lord of Ruthin, *see* Corwen (M)

Griffiths, Jane, *see* Ffestiniog (M)

Griffiths, Moses, artist, *see* Llanelltud (M)

Gruffyd ap Adda, effigy, *see* Towyn (M)

Gwaelod, fortified towns of, *see* p. 13 (C)

Gwbert, hamlet, *see* Verwick (C)

Gwerclas, house and memorials, *see* Llangar (M)

Gwniad, species of fish, *see* Bala (M)

Gwlltion Cochion Mawddwy (brigands) *see* Mallwyd (M)

Gwynedd, kingdom, *see* p. 77 (M), Ffestiniog (M)

Gwynfynydd mine, *see* Llanfachreth (M)

Gwynne, Rev. Alban, *see* Aberaeron (C), Llanbadarn Trefeglwys (C), Llanddewi Aberarth (C)

Hafod Arms Hotel, *see* Llanfihangel y Creuddyn Upper (C)

Hafod, house, *see* p. 26 (C), Llanfihangel y Creuddyn Upper (C)

Hammand, woodcarvers, *see* Llanfihangel y Creuddyn Lower (C)

Happy Valley, *see* Towyn (M)

Hardman Studios, stained glass, *see* Pontrhydfendigaid (C), Trefeirig (C)

Harford family, *see* Lampeter (C)

Harlech, *see* Llandanwg (M), castle, *see* p. 88 (M), dome, *see* p. 78 (M), Lord, *see* Talsarnau (M)

Haroldstone, house, *see* Dolgellau (M)

Harris, Howell, *see* Llangeitho (C)

Hawen, chapel and hamlet, *see* Troedyraur (C)

Hawkins, M. Rhode, architect, *see* Llangar (M)

Haycock, E., architect, *see* Barmouth (M)

Hayward, C. J., architect, *see* Aberystwyth (C)

Hayward, John, stained glass, *see* Llan-Ilwchaearn (C)

Hendwr Farm, *see* Llandrillo (M)
Hengwm Valley, *see* Aran (M)
Hengwrt, house, *see* Llanelltud (M), hotel, *see* Llanfachreth (M)
Henllan, hamlet, *see* p. 9 (C), Orllwyn (C)
Henry IV, King, *see* Corwen (M)
Henry VII King, *see* Llanarth (C)
Hermon chapel, *see* Trefilan (C)
Heslop, Thomas, tombstone, *see* Llandyfriog (C)
Heulwen, house, *see* Bala (M)
Highmead, house, *see* Llanwenog (C)
Hirnant Valley, *see* Llanfor (M)
History of Merioneth, see p. 92 (M)
Holland and Holt, stained glass, *see* Pennal (M)
Holland, Samuel, M.P., *see* Llanaber (M)
Hugh, Rowland, poet, *see* Llangower (M)
Hughes, family arms *see* Llangar (M)
Hughes, H., stained glass, *see* Llanegryn (M)
Hughes, Henry, tombstone, *see* Pontrhydfendigaid (C)
Humphrey, Norman warlord, *see* Llandyssul (C)
Humphreys, family tablet, *see* Gwyddelwern (M)
Hydro Electricity, *see* p. 9 (C), Melindwr (C)

Inglis Jones family, *see* Llangybi (C)
Innes, J. D., artist, *see* Arenig, (M)
Iron Age, *see* p. 13 (C), p. 78 (M), Llanenddwyn (M)

James, Sir David and family, *see* Pontrhydfendigaid (C)
Jeffreys, family, *see* Ysgubor Coed (C)
Jelf, Rev. W. E., *see* Llanaber (M)
Jenkins, Joseph, preacher, *see* Aberporth (C)
Jesus College, Oxford, *see* Bala (M)
John, Augustus, artist, *see* Arenig (M), Bettws Gwerfil Goch (M), Llanfor (M)
Johnes, Thomas and Mariamne *see* Llanfihangel y Creuddyn Upper (C)
Jones, A. Gwynne, artist, *see* Trefeirig (C)
Jones, and Willis, stained glass, *see* Llangelynin (M)
Jones, Ann, tombstone, *see* Llanbadarn Fawr (C)
Jones, Rev. David, tablet, *see* Llanddewi Aberarth (C)
Jones, George, architect, *see* Aberystwyth (C)
Jones, Rev. Griffith, *see* Llangeitho (C)
Jones, Rev. Humphrey, *see* Llancynfelin (C)
Jones, Inigo, *see* Llanddwywe is y Graig (M)
Jones, Jenny, *see* Talyllyn (M)
Jones John, regicide, *see* Rhinog (M)
Jones, John, of Nanteos, tablet, *see* **Llanbadarn Fawr (C)**

Jones, Rev. John, memorial window, *see* Ystrad Meurig (C)
Jones, Mary, *see* Llanfihangel y Pennant (M)
Jones, Miss, heiress, *see* Llanddewi Aberarth (C)
Jones, Rice, tablet, *see* Llanfachreth (M)
Joseph of Arimathea, *see* Llanbadarn y Creuddyn Lower (C)
Joshua, Seth, preacher, *see* Aberporth (C)

Keble, Bishop, *see* Llangorwen (C)
Kempton Park Jubilee, *see* Llanfor (M)
King, T., sculptor, *see* Troedyraur (C)
Knight family of Croft Castle, *see* Llanfihangel y Creuddyn Upper (C)

Lakes, *see* under Llyn below
Lake Gwernan Hotel, *see* Cader Idris (M)
Lasynys, house, *see* Llandanwg (M)
Lees, Derwent, artist, *see* Arenig (M)
Leir, family tablets, *see* Llanychaearn (C)
Lemmon, A. E., stained glass, *see* Silian (C)
Leri, river and valley, *see* p. 9 (C), Borth (C), Ceulany Maes Mawr (C), Tirymynach (C)
Lerry Mill, *see* Ceulany Maes Mawr (C)
Lever Gallery, Port Sunlight, *see* Llanbedr (M)
Lewis, Roy, stained glass, *see* p. 28 (C), Llandre (C)
Lisburne family, *see* Llanafan (C), Tregaron (C)
Liverpool Corporation, *see* Lampeter (C) Llanycil (M)
Llambed Forest, *see* Llanfair Clydogau (C)
Llanayron, house, *see* Ciliau Aeron (C)
Llanbendigaid, house, *see* Llangelynin (M)
Llanerch Aeron, *see* Ciliau Aeron (C)
Llanfair, hamlet, *see* Orllwyn (C)
Llanfarian, village, *see* Llanychaearn (C)
Llan Farm, *see* Llanfrothen (M)
Llanfihangel Traethu, *see* Talsarnau (M)
Llanio, *see* Llanddewi Brefi (C)
Llanllyr, house, *see* Llanfihangel Ystrad (C)
Llanon, *see* Llansantffraid (C)
Llantrisant, hamlet, *see* Llanfihangel y Creuddyn Upper (C)
Llanwnnws, hamlet, *see* Ystrad Meurig (C)
Llechryd, village, *see* Llangoedmor (C)
Llechwedd, quarries, *see* Ffestiniog (M)
Llethyr, *see* Rhinog (M)
Lletysynod, mines, *see* Llanafan (C), Llanfihangel y Creuddyn Upper (C)
Lloyd Anwil family, *see* Llanycil (M)
Lloyd families, *see* Llangoedmor (C), Llandyssul (C), Corwen (M), Llanfor (M), Llangar (M) Llanycil (M)

Lloyd George, David, *see* Llanfrothen (M)
Lloyd, Sir Thomar Davien, Bart, *see* Llangynllo (C)
Llwyd, Hugh, soldier, *see* Maentwrog (M)
Llwyd, Morgan (*The Three Birds*), *see* Maentwrog (M)
Llwyncelyn, hamlet, *see* Llanarth (C)
Llwyndafydd, hamlet, *see* Llantyssiliogogo (C)
Llwynduris, house *see* Llandygwydd (C)
Llwyngwril, village, *see* Llangelynin (M)
Llwyn y Groes, hamlet, *see* Gartheli (C)
Llyfnant Valley, *see* p. 9 (C)
Llyn Arenig, *see* Arenig (M)
Llyn Barfog, *see* Towyn (M)
Llyn Berwyn, *see* Tregaron (C)
Llyn Bodlyn, *see* Llanddwywe is y Graig (M)
Llyn Cau, *see* Cader Idris (M)
Llyn Celyn (Treweryn), *see* Llanycil (M)
Llyn Craig y Pistyll, *see* Tirymynach (C)
Llyn Crogennen, *see* Llangelynin (M)
Llyn Fanod *see* Blaenpennal (C)
Llyn Gadair, *see* Cader Idris (M)
Llyn Gafr, *see* Cader Idris (M)
Llyn Gwaith, *see* Llanfair Clydogau (C)
Llyn Gwernan, *see* Cader Idris (M)
Llyn Hywel, *see* Rhinog (M)
Llyn Llygad Rheidol, *see* Plinlimon (C), Trefeirig (C)
Llyn Mair, *see* Ffestiniog (M)
Llyn Mynyllod, *see* Llandrillo (M)
Llyn Penrhaiadr, *see* Ceulany Maes Mawr (C)
Llyn Perfeddau, *see* Rhinog (M)
Llyn Pryved, *see* Trawsfynydd (M)
Llyn Stwlan, *see* Moelwyn (M)
Llyn Tegid (Bala Lake), *see* Bala (M)
Llyn Teifi, *see* Pontrhydfendigaid (C)
Llyn Twr Glas, *see* Trawsfynnydd (M)
Llywarch Hên, *see* Llanfor (M)
Llywelyn the Great, *see* Llanfihangel y Pennant (M)
Login, hamlet and chapel, *see* Verwick (C)
Loventium, *see* Llanddewi Brefi (C)

Mabws, house, *see* Llanrhystyd Haminog (C)
Maesglas, housing estate, *see* Cardigan (C)
Maesmor, John, tablet, *see* Bettws Gwerfil Goch (M)
Maesllyn Mill, *see* Llangynllo (C)
Maestir, hamlet, *see* Lampeter (C)
Maes y Garnedd Farm, *see* Rhinog (M)
Maes y Neuadd, hotel, *see* Talsarnau (M)
Mainwaring, D., sculptor, *see* Llandyssul (C), Troedyraur (C)
Mair, chapel, *see* Llanfair Clydogau (C)
Mancini, A., sculptor, *see* Llanddewi Brefi (C)
Manganese mines, *see* p. 80 (M), Rhinog (M)
Manod, quarries, *see* Ffestiniog (M)

Manor House, Abermad, *see* Llany-chaearn (C)
Marine Terrace, *see* Towyn (M)
Martin de Tours, Norman Marcher Lord, *see* Llangynllo (C)
Mawddach estuary, *see* p. 85 (M), Llanaber (M), Llanelltud (M)
Mawddwy, *see* Aran (M)
Meirion, *see* Aran (M)
Meirion Woollen Mill, *see* Mallwyd (M)
Megaliths absence of, *see* p. 13 (C)
Melin y Wig hamlet, *see* Gwyddelwern (M)
Mendham, J. B., architect, *see* Llangelynin (M)
Merioneth Historical and Record Society, *see* p. 92 (M)
Merioneth Militia, *see* Llanfor (M)
Merton College, Oxford *see* Llanuwchllyn (M)
Meyrick, Edmund, *see* Bala (M)
Meyrick (*History and Antiquities of Cardigan*), *see* Ciliau Aeron (C)
Middleton and Prothero, architects, *see* Llandyssul (C)
Middleton and Son, architects, *see* Aberystwyth (C)
Middleton, Cheltenham, architect, *see* Llandyfriog (C)
Middleton Professor, architect, *see* Lampeter (C)
Middleton, Sir William, *see* Llanafan (C)
Milltir Cerrig, *see* Llandderfel (M)
Minerals, *see* p. 13 (C), pp. 78, 80 (M)
Ministry of Public Building & Works, *see* Llandanwg (M), Llanfihangel y Pennant (M), Llangar (M)
Ministry of Technology, *see* Aberporth (C)
Mochras Peninsula, *see* p. 82 (M), Llanenddwyn (M)
Moel Goedog, *see* p. 78 (M)
Moel Fferna, *see* Berwyn (M)
Monachty, house, *see* p. 26 (C), Llanbadarn Trefeglwys (C)
Morris, William, stained glass, *see* Llangelynin (M)
Morton, Peter, tablet, *see* Aberdovey (M)
Mountain Roads, *see* Llanddewi Brefi (C), Pontrhydfendigaid (C), Tregaron (C)
Mwnt, *see* Verwick (C)
Myddleton, Sir Thomas, *see* p. 13 (C)
Mydroilin, hamlet, *see* Llanarth (C)
Mynach, River, *see* Llanfihangel y Creuddyn Upper (C)
Mynydd Bach Forest, *see* Ystrad Meurig (C)

Nannau Hall *see* Dolgellau (M), Llanfachreth (M)
Nanney, Anne, *see* Llanfachreth (M)
Nantcol Valley, *see* Rhinog (M)
Nanteos, house, *see* p. 26 (C), Llanbadarn y Creuddyn Lower (C)
Nanternis, chapel, *see* Llantyssiliogogo (C)

Nantyarian, valley slope, *see* p. 13 (C)
Nant y Moch Reservoir, *see* p. 9 (C), Ceulany Maes Mawr (C), Melindwr (C), Plinlimon (C)
Nash, John, architect, *see* p, 9 (C), Aberaeron (C), Aberystwyth (C), Cardigan (C), Ciliau Aeron (C), Llanbadarn Trefeglwys (C), Llanfihangel y Creuddyn Upper (C), Llangoedmor (C), Penbryn (C)
Nash-Williams, Professor V. E., *see* Llanbadarn Fawr (C)
National Agricultural Advisory Service, *see* Llanafan (C)
National Library of Wales, *see* Aberystwyth (C), Llanegryn (M)
Neolithic Age, *see* p. 77 (M), dolmens, *see* Llanenddwyn (M)
Neuadd, house, *see* Llanarth (C)
Newberry, R. J., stained glass, *see* Lampeter (C)
Newcastle, Duke of, *see* Llanfihangel y Creuddyn Upper (C)
Newman, Cardinal, *see* Llangorwen (C)
Nicholson and Sons, architects, *see* Aberystwyth (C)
Norman Conquest, *see* p. 13 (C), Cardigan (C), Llandre (C), Llandyssul (C), Ysgubor Coed (C), Bala (M), Corwen (M), Maentwrog (M)
Noyadd Trefawr, house, *see* Llandygwydd (C)
Nuclear Power Station, *see* Trawsfynydd (M)

Oakley Arms Hotel, *see* Ffestiniog (M)
Oakeley, family, *see* Ffestiniog (M), Maentwrog (M), quarries, *see* Ffestiniog (M)
Oakford, hamlet, *see* Llanarth (C)
Oerddrws Pass, *see* Mallwyd (M)
Old Clergy House, *see* Corwen (M)
Ormsby Gore, family, *see* Talsarnau (M)
Outward Bound Schools, *see* Aberdovey (M)
Owain Glyndwr, *see* p. 77 (M), Corwen (M), Llandanwg (M), Llanfachreth (M), Llansantffraid Glyndwfrdwy (M), Hotel *see* Corwen (M), Mount, *see* Corwen (M)
Owen, Athelstane, *see* Aberdovey (M)
Owen family of Crafnant, *see* Llanfair (M)
Owen, Rev. Hugh, *see* Llanegryn (M)
Owen, Judge, *see* Dolgellau (M)
Owen, Matthew, poet, *see* Llanbedr (M)
Oxford Movement, *see* Llangorwen (C)

Padmore, P. M., architect, *see* Llanymawddwy (M)
Paith Valley, *see* Llanbadarn y Creuddyn Lower (C)
Pale Hall, *see* Llandderfel (M)
Palladian Stable Screen, *see* Llanbadarn y Creuddyn Lower (C)
Palmer, Samuel, artist, *see* Llanfachreth (M)
Pant Clyd, *see* Aran (M)

Pantgwyn, house, *see* Llangoedmor (C)
Pantglas, chapel, *see* Llanfor (M)
Pantyfedwen, house *see* Borth (C) farm *see* Pontrhydfendigaid (C)
Pant yr Odyn, cottages, *see* Dolgellau (M)
Pared yr Ychain, *see* Aran (M)
Parson's Bridge, *see* Cwmrheidol (C)
Peacock, Thomas L., writer, *see* p. 13 (C), (*Misfortunes of Elphin*) *see* Ceulany Maes Mawr (C), Ffestiniog (M), (*Headlong Hall*) *see* Maentwrog (M)
Pelagian Heresy, *see* Llanddewi Brefi (C)
Pen Dinas, hillforts, *see* p. 13 (C), Aberystwyth (C), p. 78 (M)
Peniarth, house, *see* Llanegryn (M)
Penmaenpool, hamlet, *see* Brithdir (M)
Pennal Towers, house, *see* Pennal (M)
Pennant, hamlet, *see* Llanbadarn Trefeglwys (C)
Penparc, chapel, *see* Cardigan (C)
Penrhiwllan, hamlet, *see* Orllwyn (C)
Penrhos, hamlet, *see* Llangar (M)
Penrhyngoch, hamlet, *see* Tirymynach (C), Trefeirig (C)
Pensarn, chapel, *see* Llantyssiliogogo (C)
Penson, R. K., architect, *see* p. 26 (C), Llangynllo (C), Llanilar (C)
Pentregat, chapel, *see* Llangranog (C)
Penuwch, hamlet, *see* Cilcennin (C), Nantcwnlle (C)
Pen y Gadair *see* Cader Idris (M)
Penylan, house, *see* Llandygwydd (C)
Petit Rev. J. L., *see* Llanaber (M)
Phillips, Katherine, poet, *see* Cardigan (C)
Phillips, Thomas, library, *see* Lampeter (C)
Picturesque, theory of, *see* p. 9 (C), Llanfihangel y Creuddyn Upper (C)
Pigeonsford, house, *see* Llangranog (C)
Pistyll y Cain, waterfall, *see* Llanfachreth (M)
Pistyll y Mawddach, waterfall, *see* Llanfachreth (M)
Plâs, house, *see* Mallwyd (M)
Plâs Brondanw, house, *see* Llanfrothen (M)
Plâs Gogerddan Plant Breeding Station *see* p. 19 (C), Trefeirig (C)
Plâs Gwernant, house, *see* Troedyraur (C)
Plâs Hên, house, *see* Brithdir (M)
Plâs Llangoedmor, house, *see* Llangoedmor (C)
Plâs Rhiw-Waedog, house, *see* Llanfor (M)
Plâs Tanybwlch, house, *see* Ffestiniog (M)
Plâs y Wern, house, *see* Llanarth (C)
Plwmp, hamlet, *see* Llantyssiliogogo (C)
Pond Syfrydin, *see* Tirymynach (C)
Pont Cerrig, *see* Rhinog (M)
Ponterwyd, village, *see* p. 11 (C), Ceulany Maes Mawr (C), Cwmrheidol (C)
Pont Gribble, *see* Trawsfynydd (M)

145

Ponthirwaun, hamlet, *see* Llandygwydd (C)

Pontrhydygroes, village, *see* p. 13 (C), Yspytty Ystwyth (C)

Pontshaen, hamlet, *see* Llandyssul (C)

Pony Track, *see* Cader Idris (M)

Port Meirion, *see* p. 90 (M), Penrhyndeudraeth (M)

Postmawr, hamlet, *see* Llanllwchaearn (C)

Pountney Smith, S., architect, *see* Llandderfel (M), Llandrillo (M)

Precipice Walks, *see* Llanelltud (M)

Prengwyn, hamlet, *see* Llandyssul (C)

Price family of Rhiwlas, *see* Llanfor (M)

Price, Sir Uvedale, *see* p. 9 (C), Aberystwyth (C)

Pritchard, M., architect, *see* Dolgellau (M)

Prothero and Phillpot, architects, *see* Aberaeron (C)

Pryse family, *see* Trefeirig (C)

Puddicombe, Anne, (*By Berwyn Banks*, etc.) *see* Penbryn (C)

Pugin, architect, *see* Llangelynin (M)

Quakers, *see* Llangelynin (M)

Quoits, *see* Llandyssul (C)

Railways, *see* Aberaeron (C), Aberystwyth (C), Cardigan (C), Llanfihangel y Creuddyn Upper (C), Ffestiniog (M), Llangelynin (M), Towyn (M)

Raine, Allen, *see* Puddicombe, Anne, above

Read, F., sculptor, *see* Llangoedmor (C)

Redheaded Men of Mawddwy, *see* Mallwyd (M)

Red Lion Hotels, *see* Llanrhystyd Mefenydd (C), Mallwyd (M)

Rees, Bishop Timothy, *see* Llanbadarn Trefeglwys (C)

Regency Architecture *see* p. 16 (C), Aberaeron (C)

Rendel, Lord, *see* Aberystwyth (C)

Rennie, John, engineer, *see* Newquay (C)

Repton, George, S. architect, *see* Aberystwyth (C)

Revivals, religious, *see* Aberporth (C), Llancynfelin (C), Llangeitho (C)

Rhagad Hall, *see* Corwen (M)

Rhaiadr Du, waterfall, *see* Llanelltud (M)

Rheidol, river, *see* p. 9 (C), Llanfihangel y Creuddyn Upper (C), Llanychaearn (C)

Rhiwlas, house, *see* Llanfor (M)

Rhoslefain, hamlet, *see* Llangelynin (M)

Rhos y Gwaliau, hamlet, *see* Llanfor (M)

Rhug, house and estate, *see* p. 91 (M), Corwen (M)

Rhydigwyn, chapel, *see* Llanfihangel Ystrad (C)

Rhydlewis, hamlet, *see* Troedyraur (C)

Rhydowen, chapel, *see* Llandyssul (C)

Rhydyfen, *see* Arenig (M)

Rhydymain, hamlet, *see* Llanfachreth (M), Rhobell (M)

Rhys ap Dafydd, Prince, *see* Ysgubor Coed (C)

Rhys, Professor Sir John, *see* Cwmrheidol (C)

Richard II, King, *see* Corwen (M)

Richard, E. schoolmaster, *see* Ystrad Meurig (C)

Richardes, Major, *see* Aberystwyth (C)

Richard, Henry, M.P. *see* Tregaron (C)

Richards family, *see* Llanychaearn (C)

Richards, Sir Richard, *see* Brithdir (M) Dolgellau (M)

Richardson, Henry, *see* Llanfor (M)

Roads, *see* p. 13 (C), p. 85 (M)

Roberts, Evan, preacher, *see* Aberporth (C)

Roberts, Robert, Life and Opinions, of travelling scholar, see p. 92 (M)

Robertson, Henry, M.P, *see* Llandderfel (M)

Robinson, P. F., architect, *see* Lampeter (C)

Rock Mill, *see* Llandyssul (C)

Rock Terrace, *see* Barmouth (M)

Roman remains, *see* p. 13 (C), Llanddewi Brefi (C), p. 78 (M), Llanuwchllyn (M), Maentwrog (M), Pennal (M)

Roman Steps, *see* Rhinog (M)

Rothschild, Lord, *see* Ffestiniog (M)

Routelli, sculptor, *see* Aberystwyth (C)

Rowlands, Rev. Daniel and family, *see* Llangeitho (C), Nantcwnlle (C)

Royal Commission Report on Ancient Monuments, see p. 92 (M)

Royal St. David's Golf Course and Hotel, *see* Llandanwg (M)

Royal Society *Transactions*, *see* Troedyraur (C)

Ruskin's Guild of St. George, *see* Barmouth (M)

Ryder, seed firm, *see* Corwen (M)

St. Cadfan, *see* Llandrillo (M), Towyn (M)

St. David, *see* Henfynyw (C), Llanddewi Brefi (C)

St. David's College, *see* Corwen (M)

St. David's University College, *see* Lampeter (C)

St. Derfel Gadern, *see* Llandderfel (M)

St. Ithel Hael, *see* Llandrillo (M)

St. Non's Chapel, *see* Llansantffraid (C)

St. Padarn, *see* Aberystwyth (C), Llanbadarn Fawr (C)

St. Trillo, *see* Llandrillo (M)

Salem, chapels, *see* Llanbedr (M), Llangar (M)

Salesbury or Salisbury family, *see* Corwen (C)

Sandmarsh Cottage, *see* Aberystwyth (C)

Sarnau, hamlets, *see* Penbryn (C), Llandderfel (M)

Sarn Helen, Roman Road, *see* Blaenpennal (C), Cellan (C), Llanbadarn Odwyn (C), Llanddewi Brefi (C), Llanfair Clydogau (C), Berwyn (M)

Savin, Thomas, *see* Aberystwyth (C)

Saxonbury Lodge, Sussex, *see* Llangeitho (C)

Scalpell, Father, *see* Dolgellau (M)

Schools, architecture and influence of, *see* p. 28 (C), Ystrad Meurig (C)

Scott, Sir Gilbert, architect, *see* Lampeter (C), Llandderfel (M)

Scott, Sir Giles Gilbert, architect, *see* Dolgellau (M)

Sedding, J., architect, *see* Brithdir (M), Dolgellau (M)

Seddon, J. P., architect, *see* Aberystwyth (C), Llanbadarn Fawr (C), Llanychaearn (C)

Seilo Chapel, *see* Aberystwyth (C)

Seithenyn ap Seithenyn Sardi, *see* p. 13 (C)

Seward, stained glass, *see* Llanfor (M)

Shell Island (Mochras), *see* Llanenddwyn (M)

Ship Inn, Pennant, *see* Llanbadarn Trefeglwys (C)

Shrigley and Hunt, stained glass, *see* Borth (C), Tregaron (C)

Siloam, chapel, *see* Verwick (C)

Sion, chapel *see* Cilcennin (C)

Skerries, *see* Llandygwydd (C)

Slate, *see* p. 80 (M), Ffestiniog (M), Moelwyn (M), Talyllyn (M)

Snowdonia National Park, *see* Llanfor (M)

Soar a Mynydd, chapel, *see* Tregaron (C)

Soar, chapel, *see* Llancynfelin (C)

Spence, Sir Basil, architect, *see* Trawsfynydd (M)

Stanley House, *see* Cardigan (C)

Stapledon, Professor G., *see* p. 19 (C), Trefeirig (C)

Stedman family, *see* Pontrhydfendigaid (C)

Stewart family, memorial window, *see* Silian (C)

Stinchcombe, Glos., *see* Llangorwen (C)

Strata Florida, *see* Pontrhydfendigaid (C)

Stuart, architect, *see* Llandyfriog (C)

Swaine Bourne, stained glass, *see* Bettws Gwerfil Goch (M)

Swinburne, A., *see* Llanbadarn y Creuddyn Lower (C)

Swyddffynon, hamlet, chapel, *see* Lledrod Issa (C)

Synod Inn, *see* Llanllwchaearn (C)

Tabernacle, chapels, *see* Cardigan (C), Llandyssul (C)

Tairvelyn, brook, *see* Llanfor (M)

Talardd, hamlet, *see* Llanuwchllyn (M)

Talbot Hotel, *see* Tregaron (C)

Talbot, Mrs., *see* Barmouth (M)

Talgarth, house, *see* Towyn (M)

Taliesin's Grave, *see* Ceulany Maes Mawr (C)

Talsarn, village, *see* Trefilan (C)

Talybont, villages, *see* p. 10 (C), Ceulany Maes Mawr (C), Llanddwywe is y Graig (M)

Talyllyn Railway Preservation Society, *see* Towyn (M)

Tanybwlch, house and station, *see* Ffestiniog (M)

Tanygrisiau, reservoir, *see* Moelwyn (M)

Teifi, river, *see* p. 9 (C), Brongwyn (C), Cardigan (C), Llandyssul (C), Pontrhydfendigaid (C), Tregaron (C)

Telford, Thomas, *see* p. 85 (M), Corwen (M)

Temple Bar, hamlet, *see* Llanfihangel Ystrad (C)

Temple, Frederick, Archbishop, *see* Dolgellau (M)

Thomas, Evan, poet, *see* Llanarth (C)

Thomas, Sir Percy and Sons, architects, *see* Aberystwyth (C)

Thomas, Rev., R. S., poet, *see* Ysgubor Coed (M)

Thompson, Lilian, memorial window, *see* Lledrod Ucha (C)

Thurston, family tablets, *see* Pennal (M)

Tomen Las, *see* Ysbugor Coed (C)

Tomen y Bala, *see* Bala (M)

Tomen y Mur, *see* p. 78 (M), Maentwrog (M)

Tonfanau, *see* Llangelynin (M)

Tooth, Rev., Charles, *see* Brithdir (M)

Torrent Walk, *see* Dolgellau (M)

Towy, river, *see* p. 11 (C), Tregaron (C)

Towyn, chapel, *see* Newquay (C)

Trade Routes, *see* p. 78 (M)

Traeth Bach, *see* Talsarnau (M)

Travers, Martin, stained glass, *see* Llancynfelin (C)

Trawscoed, house, *see* Llanafan (C), Llanbadarn y Creuddyn Lower (C)

Trefenter, hamlet, *see* Llangwryfon (C)

Treforgan, house, *see* Llangoedmor (C)

Tremain, school, *see* Verwick (C), church, *see* Llangoedmor (C)

Tre'r ddol, village, *see* Llancynfelin (C)

Tresaith, beach, *see* Penbryn (C)

Treweryn, river, *see* Bala (M), reservoir *see* Llanycil (M)

Trichrug, *see* Trefilan (C)

Troedraur House, *see* Bettws Ifan (C)

Troedyrhiw, chapel, *see* Dihewid (C), house, *see* Penbryn (C)

Trystion, valley and falls, *see* Llangar (M)

Tyglyn, house, *see* Llanddewi Aberarth (C)

Tynewydd, *see* Rhobell (M)

Tyn y Bont, chapel, *see* Llanycil (M)

Tyn y Coed, house, *see* Llangelynin (M)

Tyn y Cornel Hotel, *see* Talyllyn (M)

Tyn y Graig, chapel, *see* Ystrad Meurig (C)

Tyn y Groes Hotel, *see* Llanelltud (M)

Tyrau Mawr, *see* Cader Idris (M), Llangelynin (M)

Unitarian meeting house, *see* Aberystwyth (C), schisms, *see* Llandyssul (C)

University of Wales, *see* Aberystwyth (C), Lampeter (C

Unknown Warrior, *see* Llanuwchllyn (M)

Uppingham School, *see* Borth (C)

Urdd Gobaith Cymru (Welsh League of Youth), *see* Llangranog (C), Llanuwchllyn (M)

U.S. Flying Fortress, wreckage of, *see* Arenig (M)

Vander Hagen, sculptor, *see* Corwen (M), Llanddwywe Is y Graig (M)

Van Dyck, Sir Anthony, *see* Trefeirig (C)

Vaughan families, of Cors y Gedol, *see* Llanddwywe Is y Graig (M), of Hengwrt, Colonel, *see* Tallylyn (M), hatchment *see* Llanelltud (M), Robert, antiquary, *see* Llanelltud (M), of Nannau *see* Llanfachreth (M), of Rhug and Nannau *see* Llandderfel (M), tablets *see* Llanfihangel Ystrad (C)

Vaughan, Rowland, poet, *see* Llanuwchllyn (M)

Victoria Hotel, *see* Llanbedr (M)

Vosper, Sydney Curnow, artist, *see* Llanbedr (M)

Wagner, Richard, composer, *see* Llanbadarn y Creuddyn Lower (C)

Walking, *see* p. 82 (M)

Walter de Bec, Norman warlord, *see* Llandre (C)

Ward and Hughes, stained glass, *see* Llanfachreth, (M) Pennal (M)

Ward, Frank, *Lakes of Wales*, *see* p. 92 (M), Talyllyn (M), Trawsfynydd (M)

Watch Tower Chapel, *see* Bettws Ifan (C)

Waterfalls, *see* Llanelltud (M), Llanfachreth (M), Llangar (M)

Watkin Williams, Bishop, *see* Pennal (M)

Webb, Geoffrey, stained glass, *see* Llandrillo (M), Towyn (M)

Wellington, Duke of, *see* Aberystwyth (C)

Welsh League of Youth, *see* Llangranog (C), Llanuwchllyn (M)

Welsh Plant Breeding Station, *see* Trefeirig (C)

Welsh poetry, *see* Llanarth (C), Llanbadarn Fawr (C)

Welsh Presbyterian Youth Centre, *see* Bala (M)

Westmacott, Richard, sculptor, *see* Llangybi (C)

Westphalia, *see* Llanelltud (M)

Whippell, J., stained glass, *see* Ystrad Meurig (C)

Whisky, Welsh, *see* Llanfor (M)

Whitefriars, stained glass, *see* Borth (C), Lampeter (C), Llandre (C), Llangeitho (C), Pontrhydfendigaid (C) Silian (C), Tregaron (C)

White Lion Hotels, *see* Ceulany Maes Mawr (C), Bala (M)

Wilkinson, Walter, stained glass, *see* Cardigan (C)

Williams, David J., (Smith) *see* Llanuwchllyn (M)

Williams Ellis, Clough and family, *see* Brithdir (M), Ffestiniog (M), Llanfor (M), Penrhyndeudraeth (M)

Williams, Rev. Isaac, *see* Llangorwen (C)

Williams, John, *see* Ystrad Meurig (C)

Williams, J. Lloyd, F.S.A., *see* Troedyraur (C)

Williams Wynn family of Ruabon, *see* Llanuwchllyn (M)

Wilson, Harry, architect, *see* Brithdir (M)

Wilson, Richard, artist, *see* p. 82 (M), Cader Idris (M)

Withers, R. J., architect, *see* p. 26 (C), Aberporth (C), Lampeter (C), Llanarth (C), Llandygwydd (C), Llanfihangel Ystrad (C), Llangoedmor (C), Llanllwchaearn (C), Silian (C), Trefilan (C), Yspytty Ystwyth (C)

Wnion, valley and river, *see* p. 85 (M), Aran (M), Dolgellau (M), Llanfachreth (M)

Wood, Abram, Gypsy King, *see* Llangelynin (M)

Wood, sculptor, *see* Llanbadarn Fawr (C)

Woodyer, H., stained glass, *see* Verwick (C)

Woollen Industry, *see* p. 9 (C)

Woollen Mills, *see* Ceulany Maes Mawr (C), Llandyssul (C), Llangynllo (C), Mallwyd (M)

Wordsworth, William, *see* Llanfihangel y Creuddyn Upper (C)

Wyatt, James, architect, *see* Llanfihangel y Creuddyn Upper (C)

Wyatt, T. H., architect, *see* Corwen (M)

Wynne, Rev. Ellis (*Y Bardd Cwsg*), *see* Llandanwg (M)

Wynne, Owen Slaney, of Peniarth, *see* Llanegryn (M)

Wynne, R., sculptor, *see* Llanbadarn Fawr (C)

Wynne, tomb, *see* Llandrillo (M)

Wynne, William and Katherine, *see* Talsarnau (M)

Wynne, W. W. E, of Peniarth, *see* Llanaber (M), Llanegryn (M), Towyn (M)

Y Bardd Cwsg (*The Poet Asleep*) see Llandanwg

Youth Hostels, *see* Cwmrheidol (C), Tregaron (C)

Ynysfergi Farm, *see* Borth (M)

Ynysfor, house, *see* Llanfrothen (M)

Ynys Las, *see* Borth (C)

Ynysmaengwyn, house, *see* Towyn (M)

Ysgethin River, *see* Llanddwywe is y Graig (M)

Yspytty Cynfyn, *see* Cwmrheidol (C)

Ystradgwyn, *see* Cader Idris (M)

Ystumtuen, hamlet, *see* Cwmrheidol (C)

Ystwyth Forest and River, *see* p. 13 (C), Aberystwyth (C), Llanafan (C), Llanfihangel y Creuddyn Upper (C)

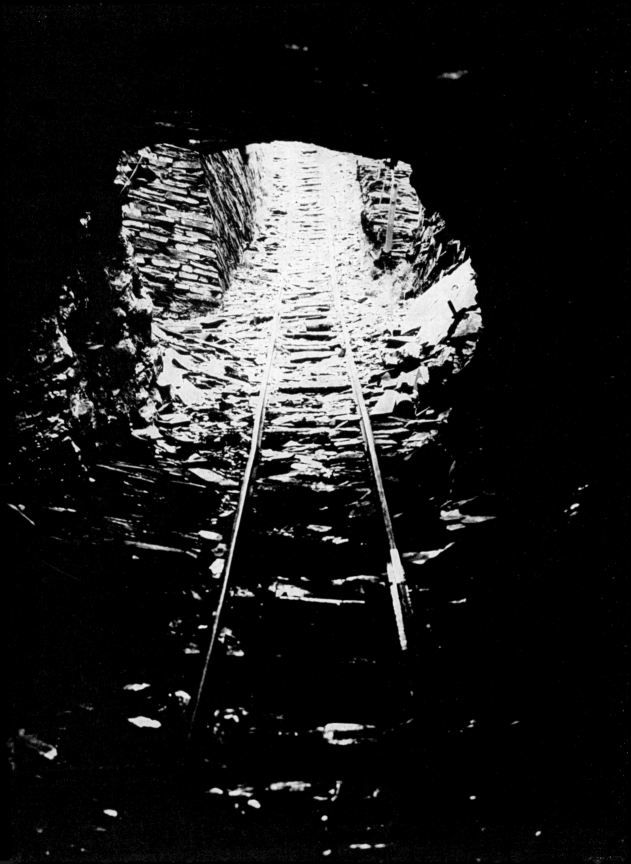